GREAT WRITING

Foundations

KEITH S. FOLSE
UNIVERSITY OF CENTRAL FLORIDA

NATIONAL GEOGRAPHIC LEARNING | CENGAGE Learning

Australia • Canada • Mexico • Singapore • Spain • United Kingdom • United States

Great Writing: Foundations
Keith S. Folse

Publisher: Sherrise Roehr

Executive Editor: Laura Le Dréan

Development Editors: Kathleen Smith,
Charlotte Sturdy

Director of Global Marketing: Ian Martin

Product Marketing Manager: Emily Stewart

International Marketing Manager:
Caitlin Thomas

Director of Content and Media Production:
Michael Burggren

Senior Content Project Manager: Daisy Sosa

Senior Print Buyer: Mary Beth Hennebury

Cover Design: Christopher Roy and
Michael Rosenquest

Cover Image: Alex Saberi/National Geographic
Stock

Interior Design: Aysling Design

Composition: PreMediaGlobal, Inc.

U.S. Edition

ISBN-13: 978-1-285-19498-1

International Student Edition

ISBN-13: 978-1-285-75064-4

National Geographic Learning/Cengage Learning
20 Channel Center Street
Boston, MA 02210
USA

Cengage learning is a leading provider of customized learning solutions with office locations around the globe, including Singapore, the United Kingdom, Australia, Mexico, Brazil, and Japan. Locate our local office at: **International.cengage.com/region**

Cengage Learning products are represented in Canada by Nelson Education, Ltd.

Visit NGL online at **NGL.Cengage.com**

Visit our corporate website at **cengage.com**

Printed in the United States of America
1 2 3 4 5 6 7 8 15 14 13

Contents

Scope and Sequence

Unit	Grammar for Writing	Building Vocabulary and Spelling	Original Student Writing
1 p. 2 **SENTENCES**	• Subjects and verbs • Periods and question marks • Capital letters	Words with the sound of **a** in **cat**	• Writing about you and your family • Peer editing
2 p. 18 **NOUNS**	• Singular and plural nouns • Proper nouns	Words with the sound of **e** in **bed**	• Writing about your classmates or friends • Peer editing
3 p. 34 **VERBS: SIMPLE PRESENT TENSE**	• Two verb forms: -s and no -s • Spelling verbs with –es and –ies • Irregular verbs: be and have • Negative of verbs	Words with the sound of **i** in **fish**	• Writing about things that people usually do • Peer editing
4 p. 56 **ADJECTIVES**	• Descriptive, possessive, and demonstrative adjectives • Nouns working as adjectives	Words with the sound of **o** in **hot**	• Writing about places around the world • Peer editing
5 p. 76 **VERBS: SIMPLE PRESENT TENSE OF *BE***	• The verb be • Negative of be • Sentences with be	Words with the sound of **u** in **cup**	• Writing about two cities in the same country • Peer editing
6 p. 94 **PRONOUNS**	• Subject and object pronouns	Words with the sound of **a** in **cake**	• Writing about people and their jobs • Peer editing
7 p. 112 **THE CONJUNCTION *AND***	• *And* with two words • *And* with three or more words	Words with the sound of **e** in **eat**	• Writing about your schedule for next week • Peer editing
8 p. 132 **ARTICLES: *A, AN, THE*, ---**	• Articles with singular and plural count and non-count nouns • Choosing *a* or *an* • *The* with places	Words with the sound of **i** in **rice**	• Writing about how to make a kind of food • Peer editing

Overview

Framed by engaging **National Geographic** images, this new edition of the *Great Writing* series helps students write better sentences, paragraphs, and essays. The new *Foundations* level meets the needs of low level learners through basic vocabulary development and spelling practice, and all levels feature clear explanations applied directly to appropriate practice opportunities. The *Great Writing* series is ideal for beginning to advanced learners, helping them develop and master academic writing skills.

Great Writing: Foundations focuses on basic sentence construction, emphasizing grammar, vocabulary, spelling, and composition.

Great Writing 1 focuses on sentences as they appear in paragraphs.

Great Writing 2 teaches paragraph development.

Great Writing 3 transitions from paragraphs to essays.

Great Writing 4 focuses on essays.

Great Writing 5 practices more advanced essays.

Great Writing: Foundations is the all-new introductory level of the *Great Writing* series. It is a book for beginning students of English who need more practice in forming basic sentences. To help these learners, this text provides more than 300 activities on sentence structure, grammar, spelling, vocabulary, and editing. Although the book practices writing, it is an excellent tool for improving any student's basic English skills.

From the Author

The story behind *Great Writing: Foundations*

I have taught thousands of students from all over the world. I have also been a student of several foreign languages, namely French, Spanish, Arabic, Malay, German, and Japanese. Three key areas immediately come to mind that highlight my difficulties in learning these languages: grammar, vocabulary, and writing.

The first area that most teachers recognize as a challenge to learners is grammar, or sentence structure. Each language has different rules that govern the written and/or spoken word. For example, Arabic has no *be* verb in present tense but does in past tense, Malay has no verb tenses, Japanese adjectives can have a past tense form, and German verbs usually come at the end of a sentence. These are but a few of the challenging linguistic facts I had to deal with as a language learner, yet they highlight some things our students must face as they learn English structures.

The second challenge is with vocabulary, which many people could argue is the most essential component in mastering a new language. Simply put, without words, you have no communication at all. Realizing the importance of vocabulary is one thing, but mastering the thousands of words needed is perhaps the most daunting task facing any foreign language learner. In each language that I studied, I struggled with the number of new words to be learned. Spanish, French, and German share many cognates with English, yet I still had to learn thousands of new vocabulary words and expressions. Though Japanese does have some English cognates, they are pronounced so differently that I hardly ever recognize them at first listening. In contrast, Malay and Arabic have fewer cognates. The need for extensive practice with vocabulary is critical to building communication skills in any language.

Finally, in languages where I did not know the writing system or alphabet, I struggled with writing words and ideas, not to mention sentences and paragraphs. In class, it took me a long time to copy from the board and take notes that were clear and useful for studying. I also struggled with hearing and distinguishing sounds, which made writing and understanding words very frustrating. I know firsthand how challenging learning a language can be for students who come from a different writing system, and I realize that careful and scaffolded instruction is critical to success.

Though the bulk of my work is now in training future teachers of ESL and EFL, I recently taught a low-level writing class with mostly Arabic and Spanish-speaking students. I quickly realized that I needed a different approach to teaching writing to this particular proficiency level. At this foundation level, all students need practice with sentence structure and vocabulary, but some groups need more emphasis on spelling along with vocabulary and sentence structure.

I found myself preparing new exercises for each lesson, sometimes to supplement the book I had been assigned to use, but often to replace the limited material. Thus, the rationale for *Great Writing: Foundations* is based on my years of experience teaching writing to students all over the world, but more important, it represents the difficulties that anyone learning a very different writing system faces in a new language classroom.

Overview of *Great Writing: Foundations*

Great Writing: Foundations has 14 units; each one offers approximately 20 activities. Each unit has three distinct sections: (1) Grammar for Writing, (2) Building Vocabulary and Spelling, and (3) Original Student Writing. Each unit opens with an impactful photo, which engages students in the writing topic, and a list of the unit objectives.

1. Grammar for Writing

Each unit has a specific grammatical focus that helps beginning writers build better sentences. Examples of sentence structure covered in this section of each unit include parts of speech (e.g., noun, verb, adjective, adverb, pronoun, conjunction, preposition), verb tenses (simple present, simple past, present progressive), punctuation (periods, commas for items in a series, commas with certain conjunctions), capitalization, and sentence types (simple, compound, complex).

Grammar is explained in language that is appropriate for beginning-level writers. Simple charts of grammatical forms give learners easy-to-understand access to the structures they will be using in their writing. Numerous examples are given of both correct language and incorrect language, and learners are encouraged to notice the gap between the two.

Grammar for Writing consists of 10 to 15 activities. The following features always appear in this section of a unit:

- grammar lessons with multiple examples

- rules written in student-accessible language

- identification of key grammar items in sentences

- selection of correct grammatical forms

- writing sentences using the grammar focus

- scrambled sentences

- correcting mistakes in sentences

- dictation of sentences practicing target spelling, vocabulary, and grammar

- practicing grammar and vocabulary in model writing

- guided writing: making changes in model writing

2. Building Vocabulary and Spelling

This section of each unit is built around one of the fourteen vowel sounds in English. These fourteen sounds are represented in these example words: *c_at, b_ed, f_ish, h_ot, c_up, c_ake, _eat, r_ice, hell_o, sch_ool, str_aw, w_ood, fl_ower,* and *b_oy*. While certain consonants present spelling problems (e.g., *b/v* for Spanish speakers, *b/p* for Arabic speakers, and *s/sh* for Japanese speakers), vowel spelling errors are made by almost all language groups learning English. Therefore, in each unit this section focuses on one vowel sound, but difficult consonants are routinely practiced in all units.

Each unit has a list of approximately 40 words that represent the targeted vowel sound. These words are arranged in groups according to the variant spellings and include the most frequent or most useful words selected from the Spelling Vocabulary List (Folse, 2013). For example, Unit 2 focuses on three spellings of the /ɜ/ sound as in the words *b_ed, r_eady,* and *m_any*.

A list of words can be a very useful tool (Folse, 2004), but a list is not enough for our students to learn words well enough to use them freely. Therefore, Building Vocabulary and Spelling always consists of these eight supporting activities:

- identifying words in a common words list
- matching of words and pictures
- completion of words with the targeted vowel sound
- writing sentences with spelling vocabulary in context
- scrambled letters
- dictation of words practicing target spelling
- recognition of the targeted sound next to a confusing spelling (e.g., *many / meny*)
- cumulative spelling review of all spellings thus far (e.g., *many / meny / mainy / miny*)

In addition, it is important to encourage students to get a separate notebook and to write all of their new vocabulary words in it. This Vocabulary Notebook will be an important tool for them to learn and review new English words and phrases that will help them become better writers. See page 291 for more information on keeping a Vocabulary Notebook.

3. Original Student Writing

The last section of each unit provides a writing prompt and student writing guidelines to elicit and inform original student writing. The topic of the prompt is related to one or two writing activities in Part 1 of the same unit.

Original Student Writing always consists of these two activities:

- Writing Your Ideas in Sentences or a Paragraph, which connects the content of the unit and the opening photograph
- Peer Editing (A specific Peer Editing Sheet relevant to the language and writing prompt in each unit is available online at NGL.Cengage.com/GWF. You can also see a sample in Appendix 3 on pages 297–298.)

In addition, Appendix 2 includes 140 additional topics for writing. These are optional activities, but are a good resource for daily writing practice. The more students write, the better writers they become.

Ancillary Components

In addition to the *Great Writing: Foundations* Student Book, the following components help both the instructor and the students expand their learning and teaching.

- **Online Workbook at NGL.Cengage.com/GWF**: Includes a wealth of vocabulary, grammar, spelling, writing, and editing practice with immediate feedback.

- **eBook**: Offers an interactive option.

- **Assessment CD-ROM with Exam***View*®***:** Allows instructors to create and customize tests.

- **Presentation Tool CD-ROM**: Offers instructors the ability to lead whole-class presentations and demonstrate the editing process.

- **Audio CDs**: Contains all dictation sentences and spelling lists.

- **Online Teacher's Notes and an Answer Key with Audioscripts**: Includes all answers to Student Book activities.

Works Cited

Folse, K. (2004). *Vocabulary Myths: Applying Second Language Research to Classroom Teaching.* Ann Arbor, MI: University of Michigan Press.

Folse, K. (2013, April). *The Creation of a New ESL Spelling Vocabulary List.* Paper presented at the Oman 13th International ELT Conference, Muscat, Oman.

Inside a Unit *Great Writing: Foundations*

Great Writing: Foundations is the all-new introductory level of the *Great Writing* series. It is a book for beginning students of English who need more practice in forming basic sentences. To help these learners, this text provides over 300 activities on sentence structure, grammar, spelling, vocabulary, and editing. Although the book practices writing, it is an excellent tool for improving any student's basic English accuracy and fluency skills.

—Dr. Keith Folse

Impactful **National Geographic** images open every unit and help to stimulate student writing

Grammar for Writing

Clear charts present the beginning-level structures needed to support the writing goals.

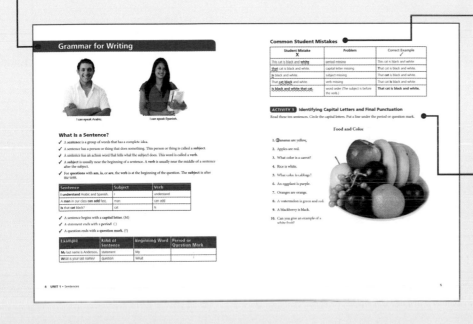

Common Student Mistakes are highlighted, and learners are encouraged to compare and contrast the differences to learn best writing practices.

10 to 15 grammar activities per unit reinforce the grammar presentation and provide opportunities to build writing skills in a logical, step-by-step manner.

Inside a Unit · *Great Writing: Foundations*

Contextualized Activities model good sentences and form the basis for the writing students do at the end of the unit.

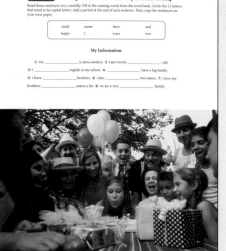

Building Vocabulary and Spelling

A focus on word lists that represent targeted vowel sounds helps beginning learners master spelling, comprehension, and pronunciation.

Common Words have been chosen due to high-frequency and usefulness.

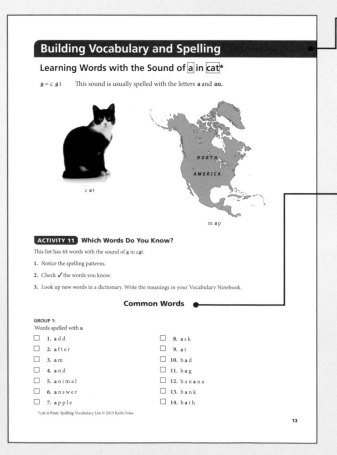

Original Student Writing

Writing prompts encourage students to combine the grammar, vocabulary, spelling, and writing skills from the unit into one writing piece.

Original Student Writing

Writing Your Ideas in Sentences or a Paragraph

Write five to ten sentences on your own paper. Write about things that people usually do. Use simple present tense. For help, you can follow the examples in Activity 11 (page 47) for one person or Activity 12 (page 48) for two or more people. (For more information about writing a paragraph, go to Appendix 4.)

Peer Editing

Exchange papers from the above activity. Read your partner's sentences. Then use Peer Editing Sheet 3 to make comments about the writing. Go to NGL.Cengage.com/GWF. There is a sample in Appendix 3.

🖥 For more practice with the **writing** in this unit, go to NGL.Cengage.com/GWF.

Writing Your Ideas in Sentences or a Paragraph provides a prompt and writing guidelines to elicit original student writing. The writing topic relates to the opening photograph and recycles the vocabulary practiced in the unit.

Peer Editing activities increase student awareness and encourage learners to become better writers.

Point-of-use **Peer Editing Sheets** provide additional editing practice. They are available online at NGL.Cengage. com/GWF.

Great Writing: Foundations Peer Editing Sheets
UNIT 1 PEER EDITING SHEET

Your name: _____

Your partner's name: _____

Date: _____

1 How many sentences did your partner write? _____

2. Does every sentence begin with a capital letter? _____

   If not, copy the sentences here that need a capital letter.

   _____

   _____

3. Does every sentence end with a period? _____

   If not, copy the sentences here that need a period.

   _____

   _____

4. Does every sentence have a subject? _____

   If not, which sentences need a subject? Copy them here.

   _____

   _____

5. Does every sentence have a verb? _____

   If not, which sentences need a verb? Copy them here.

   _____

   _____

6. Does every sentence have correct word order? _____

   If not, copy the sentences here that do not have correct word order.

   _____

   _____

Technology *Great Writing: Foundations*

For Instructors:

Assessment CD-ROM with Exam*View*® allows instructors to create and customize tests and quizzes easily.

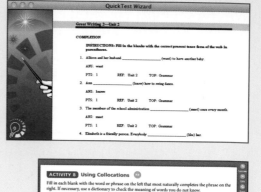

The Classroom Presentation Tool for each level contains editing activities from the Student Book. Available on CD-ROM, it makes instruction clearer and learning easier through editing activities, sentence-building activities, and grammar presentations.

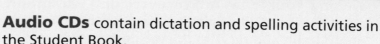
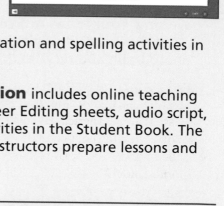

Audio CDs contain dictation and spelling activities in the Student Book.

Online Teacher's Edition includes online teaching notes for each activity, Peer Editing sheets, audio script, and answer keys for activities in the Student Book. The Teacher's Edition helps instructors prepare lessons and teach effectively.

For Students:

Online Workbook: Powered by MyELT, the **Online Workbook** is an independent student resource that supports the lessons taught in the Student Book. It includes additional vocabulary, grammar, spelling, writing, and editing practice with automatic grading for immediate feedback.

***Great Writing: Foundations* eBook** is available for an interactive, online experience, and will work on iPads, laptops, and smart phones.

Acknowledgements

I am grateful to the many people who have worked so hard on the development and production of *Foundations*, including Kathleen Smith, Laura Le Dréan, Tom Jefferies, Charlotte Sturdy, Ian Martin, and Emily Stewart, as well as for those who have given me invaluable feedback regarding this book within the series, including Beatrix Mellauner, Linda Babat, Dawn Blodgett, Nichol Clark, and Cindy Le. Ultimately, everyone's ideas and feedback have been instrumental in the design of this work.

Special thanks go to these five individuals who gave input to the design of the content of *Great Writing: Foundations*:

Mary Barratt, Iowa State University, Iowa
Laura Taylor, Iowa State University, Iowa
Abdelhay Belkafir, University of Central Florida, Florida
Taoufik Ferjani, Zayed University, United Arab Emirates
Shirley Andrews, Lafayette Parish Schools, Lafayette, Louisiana

Many thanks to the following reviewers who offered ideas and suggestions that shaped the new edition of the *Great Writing* series:

Cheryl Acorn, Pasadena City College, California
Paul McGarry, Santa Barbara City College, California
Fernanda Ortiz, University of Arizona, Arizona
Michelle Jeffries, University of Arkansas – Fayetteville, Arkansas
Suzanne Medina, California State University - Dominguez Hills, California
Kristi Miller, American English Institute, California
Kevin Van Houten, Glendale Community College, California
Izabella Kojic-Sabo, University of Windsor, Canada
Wayne Fong, Aston School, China
Yiwei Shu, New Oriental School, China
Raul Billini, John F. Kennedy Institute of Languages, Dominican Republic
Rosa Vasquez, John F. Kennedy Institute of Languages, Dominican Republic
Mike Sfiropoulos, Palm Beach State College, Florida
Louise Gobron, Georgia State University, Georgia
Gabriella Cambiasso, City College of Chicago - Harold Washington, Illinois
Kuei-ping Hsu, National Tsing Hua University, Taiwan
Morris Huang, National Taiwan University of Science and Technology, Taiwan
Cheng-Che Lin, Tainan University of Technology, Taiwan
Rita Yeh, Chia Nan University of Pharmacy and Science, Taiwan
Nguyen Chanh Tri, Vietnam Australia International School, Vietnam
Mai Minh Tien, Vietnam Australia International School, Vietnam
Tuan Nguyen, Vietnam Australia International School, Vietnam
Nguyen Thi Thanh The, Vietnam Australia International School, Vietnam
Nguyen Vu Minh Phuong, Vietnam Australia International School, Vietnam
Colleen Comidy, Seattle Central Community College, Washington
Cindy Etter, University of Washington, Washington
Kris Hardy, Seattle Central Community College, Washington
Liese Rajesh, Seattle Central Community College, Washington

Photo Credits

Unit 1

Pages 2–3: © Marshall Ikonography/ Alamy

Page 4: © Zurijeta/Shutterstock; Left: © Andresr/Shutterstock.com; Right

Page 5: © Sarah2/Shutterstock.com

Page 6: © Africa Studio/Shutterstock. com: © bajinda/Shutterstock: Andrzej

Tokarski/Shutterstock.com: picamaniac/Shutterstock.com: JIANG HONGYAN/Shutterstock. com: Tatiana Popova/Shutterstock. com: Loskutnikov/Shutterstock. com: Nataliia Melnychuk/ Shutterstock.com

Page 8: Cuson/Shutterstock.com

Page 11: © Blend Images/Alamy

Page 13: © Viorel Sima/Shutterstock. com; Left

Page 14: © Valentina R./ Shutterstock.com; Top left: © Valentina R./Shutterstock. com; Top right: © Mike Powell/ Getty Images; Bottom left: © LJSphotography/Alamy; Bottom right

Page 15: © Blend Images/Alamy; Top left: © Cameramannz/Shutterstock. com; Bottom left

Unit 2

Pages 18–19: © Mauricio Abreu/JAI/ Corbis

Page 20: © Jeanne Provost/ Shutterstock.com; Top left: © zcw/ Shutterstock.com; Top right: © catmanc/Shutterstock.com; Bottom right

Page 26: © Comstock/Photos.com

Page 28: © vvoe/Shutterstock. com; Top left: © Radu Razvan/ Shutterstock.com; Top right

Page 30: © monticello/Shutterstock. com; Top left: © Blend Images/ Alamy; Bottom right

Page 31: © Justin Kase z11z/Alamy; Bottom left: © MSPhotographic/ Shutterstock.com; Bottom right

Unit 3

Pages 34–35: © Felix Hug/Getty Images

Page 37: © Stokkete/Shutterstock. com

Page 38: © Tim_Booth/Shutterstock. com: © J.E. Mous/Shutterstock. com: © Corbis Super RF/Alamy: © Anna Kucherova/Shutterstock. com: © thumb/iStockphoto. com: © LilKar/Shutterstock.com: © Juniors Bildarchiv GmbH/ Alamy

Page 41: © Blend Images/Alamy

Page 42: © Robert Kneschke/ Shutterstock.com

Page 45: © Blend Images/Alamy

Page 47: © Jim Craigmyle/Corbis/ Glow Images

Page 49: © cbpix/Shutterstock. com; Top left: © Jan-Dirk Hansen/ Shutterstock.com; Top right

Page 50: © Bochkarev Photography/ Shutterstock.com; Top left: © digitalskillet/iStockphoto. com; Top right: © Scott Hales/ Shutterstock.com; Bottom left

Page 51: © Paul Bradbury/Alamy Limited; Top left: © Sandra Baker/ Alamy; Top right: © Igor Borodin/ Shutterstock.com; Bottom left: © John Kasawa/Shutterstock.com; Bottom right

Unit 4

Pages 56–57: © AUNG PYAE SOE/ National Geographic Creative

Page 58: © Jan-Dirk Hansen/ Shutterstock.com; Top left: © Songquan Deng/Alamy; Top right

Page 62: © Derek Cole/Photolibrary/ Getty Images

Page 66: © Figurative Speech/Getty Images

Page 67: © philipus/Alamy Limited; inset

Page 70: © Joe Belanger/ Shutterstock.com; Top left: © Musician/Shutterstock.com; Top middle: © RJ Lerich/Shutterstock. com; Top right

Page 71: © James A. Harris/ Shutterstock.com: © Michael N Paras/Getty Images: © Crepesoles/ Shutterstock.com: © Ronald Sumners/Shutterstock.com: © Musician/Shutterstock.com: © David Gunn/iStockphoto.com: Grigoryeva Liubov Dmitrievna/ Shutterstock.com: © Serdar Tibet/ Shutterstock.com

Unit 5

Pages 76–77: © Scott Markewitz/ Photographer's Choice/Getty Images

Page 78: © Pavel Losevsky/Fotolia LLC; Top: © dotstock/Shutterstock. com; Bottom left: © Takayuki/ Shutterstock.com; Middle left: © Werner Buchel/Shutterstock. com; Middle right: © Comstock Images/Thinkstock; Bottom right

Page 79: © Jupiterimages/Brand X Pictures/Thinkstock; Top left: © Smart-foto/Shutterstock.com; Top middle left: © gulfimages/ Alamy; Top middle right: © Megapress/Alamy; Top right

Page 84: © AMY TOENSING/ National Geographic Creative

Page 87: © tlorna/Shutterstock.com; Top left; © Jean-Yves Benedeyt/ iStockphoto.com; Middle

UNIT 1

Sentences

A family visits Lake Louise Banff National Park, Alberta, Canada.

OBJECTIVES **Grammar:** To learn about word order in a sentence
Vocabulary and Spelling: To study common words with the sound of <u>a</u> in c<u>a</u>t
Writing: To write about you and your family

Can you write about you and your family?

Grammar for Writing

I can speak Arabic.

I can speak Spanish.

What Is a Sentence?

✓ A **sentence** is a group of words that has a complete idea.

✓ A sentence has a person or thing that does something. This person or thing is called a **subject**.

✓ A sentence has an action word that tells what the subject does. This word is called a **verb**.

✓ A **subject** is usually near the beginning of a sentence. A **verb** is usually near the middle of a sentence after the subject.

✓ For **questions** with **am**, **is**, or **are**, the **verb** is at the beginning of the question. The **subject** is after the verb.

Sentence	Subject	Verb
I understand Arabic and Spanish.	I	understand
A **man** in our class **can add** fast.	man	can add
Is that **cat** black?	cat	Is

✓ A sentence begins with a **capital letter.** (M)

✓ A statement ends with a **period.** (.)

✓ A question ends with a **question mark.** (?)

Example	Kind of Sentence	Beginning Word	Period or Question Mark
My last name is Anderson.	statement	My	.
What is your last name?	question	What	?

Common Student Mistakes

Student Mistake X	Problem	Correct Example ✓
This cat is black and **white**	period missing	This cat is black and white**.**
that cat is black and white.	capital letter missing	**T**hat cat is black and white.
Is black and white.	subject missing	That **cat** is black and white.
That **cat black** and white.	verb missing	That cat **is** black and white.
Is black and white that cat.	word order (The subject is before the verb.)	**That cat is black and white.**

ACTIVITY 1 Identifying Capital Letters and Final Punctuation

Read these ten sentences. Circle the capital letters. Put a line under the period or question mark.

Food and Color

1. Ⓑananas are yellow.

2. Apples are red.

3. What color is a carrot?

4. Rice is white.

5. What color is cabbage?

6. An eggplant is purple.

7. Oranges are orange.

8. A watermelon is green and red.

9. A blackberry is black.

10. Can you give an example of a white fruit?

Writing Sentences

Write the sentences from Activity 1 that match the correct pictures. Use a capital letter. Add a period or a question mark.

Food and Color

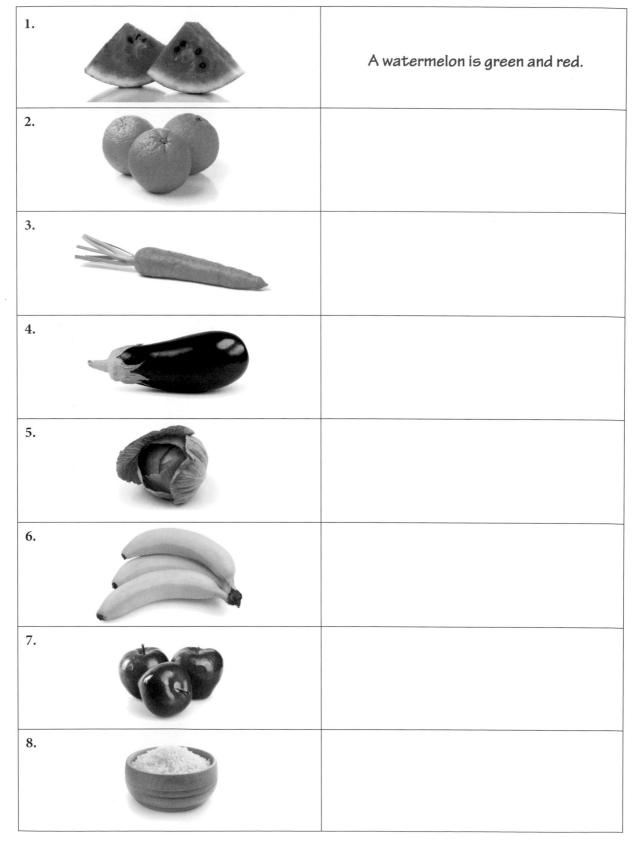

1.	A watermelon is green and red.
2.	
3.	
4.	
5.	
6.	
7.	
8.	

ACTIVITY 3 Writing Sentences about Your Information

Write your correct information in each sentence. Then write each sentence on the line. Begin with a capital letter. Use a period at the end.

About Me

1. my first name is ....

   _____

2. my first name has .... letters

   _____

3. my last name is ....

   _____

4. my last name has .... letters

   _____

5. i am .... years old

   _____

6. i am from ....

   _____

7. my favorite food is ....

   _____

8. my favorite color is ....

   _____

9. my favorite movie is ....

   _____

10. I like to .... in my free time

    _____

Read these sentences. Put one line under the subject and two lines under the verb. Then write the subjects and verbs in the correct boxes.

Sentence	Subject	Verb
1. My last <u>name</u> <u><u>has</u></u> five letters.	name	has
2. My last name is Adams.		
3. My first name is Ann.		
4. My first name has just three letters.		
5. I come from Canada.		
6. My family and I live in Toronto.		
7. I like to eat watermelons, apples, lemons, and oranges.		
8. A watermelon is green and red.		
9. Apples are red, yellow, or green.		
10. Lemons are yellow.		
11. An orange is orange.		
12. My favorite food is salad.		

ACTIVITY 5 **Writing Sentences with Correct Word Order**

Change the order of the words to write a sentence. Begin the sentence with a capital letter. End the sentence with a period.

A Talking Animal

1. <u>This animal is a bird .</u>

   animal This a is bird

2. _____

   a parrot It is

3. _____

   This colors has parrot five

4. _____

   The red and white head is

5. _____

   beautiful bird very is This

6. _____

   It smart bird very is a

7. _____

   can This talk parrot

8. _____

   can This parrot speak English

ACTIVITY 6 Scrambled Sentences

Change the order of the words to write a correct sentence. Be careful with spelling, capital letters, punctuation (.), and word order.

1. my name alex is

   _____

2. a student i am

   _____

3. i english study

   _____

4. not is so good english my

   _____

5. i my like class very much english

   _____

Circle the ten mistakes. Then write the sentences correctly. The number in parentheses ( ) is the number of mistakes in that sentence. Be ready to explain your answers.

Salad

1. (Mi) favorite (food salad.) (2)

   My favorite food is salad .
   _____

2. I lik salad with tomatoes (2)

   _____

3. i also like tuna salad (2)

   _____

4. tuna salad is very good. (1)

   _____

5. tuna salad with Apples is good. (2)

   _____

6. I like salad a lot (1)

   _____

CD 1,
Track 1 •))) **ACTIVITY 8** **Dictation**

You will hear six sentences three times. Listen carefully and write the six sentences. The number in parentheses ( ) is the number of words in the sentence. Be careful with capital letters and end punctuation.

1. _____ (6)

2. _____ (6)

3. _____ (3)

4. _____ (5)

5. _____ (6)

6. _____ (5)

Read these sentences very carefully. Fill in the missing words from the word bank. Circle the 11 letters that need to be capital letters. Add a period at the end of each sentence. Then copy the sentences on your own paper.

study	name	have	and
happy	I	years	two

My Information

1 my _____ is anna sanders. **2** **i a**m twenty _____ old.

3 i _____ english at my school. **4** _____ have a big family.

5 i have _____ brothers. **6** i also _____ two sisters. **7** i love my

brothers _____ sisters a lot. **8** we are a very _____ family.

ACTIVITY 10 Guided Writing: Making Changes in Model Writing

Write the sentences from Activity 9 again, but make the changes listed below. Sometimes you will have to make other changes, too.

<u>Sentence 1.</u> Change **Anna** to **David.**

<u>Sentence 2.</u> Change **twenty** to **sixteen.**

<u>Sentence 3.</u> Change **school** to **high school.**

<u>Sentence 4.</u> Add the word **very** in the correct place.

<u>Sentence 5.</u> Change the word **two** to **three, four,** or **five.**
Instead, you can choose a different number that you think is good for this information.

_____

_____

_____

_____

_____

_____

_____

_____

_____

_____

For more practice with the **grammar** in this unit, go to NGL.Cengage.com/GWF.

Building Vocabulary and Spelling

Learning Words with the Sound of a in cat*

a = c **a** t   This sound is usually spelled with the letters **a** and **au.**

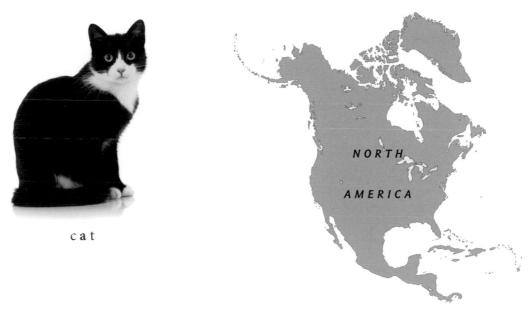

c a t

m a p

ACTIVITY 11 **Which Words Do You Know?**

This list has 44 words with the sound of **a** in c**a**t.

1. Notice the spelling patterns.

2. Check ✓ the words you know.

3. Look up new words in a dictionary. Write the meanings in your Vocabulary Notebook.

Common Words

GROUP 1:
Words spelled with **a**

☐ 1. a d d	☐ 8. a s k
☐ 2. a f t e r	☐ 9. a t
☐ 3. a m	☐ 10. b a d
☐ 4. a n d	☐ 11. b a g
☐ 5. a n i m a l	☐ 12. b a n a n a
☐ 6. a n s w e r	☐ 13. b a n k
☐ 7. a p p l e	☐ 14. b a t h

*List is from: Spelling Vocabulary List © 2013 Keith Folse

☐ 15. b l a c k   ☐ 31. l a s t

☐ 16. c a n   ☐ 32. m a n

☐ 17. c a t   ☐ 33. m a p

☐ 18. c l a s s   ☐ 34. m a t h

☐ 19. e x a m p l e   ☐ 35. n a p

☐ 20. f a m i l y   ☐ 36. s a d

☐ 21. f a s t   ☐ 37. s a l a d

☐ 22. f l a g   ☐ 38. t a x i

☐ 23. g l a s s   ☐ 39. t h a t

☐ 24. h a n d   ☐ 40. t h a n k

☐ 25. h a p p e n   ☐ 41. t r a v e l

☐ 26. h a p p y   ☐ 42. u n d e r s t a n d

☐ 27. h a s

☐ 28. h a v e   **GROUP 2:**
Words spelled with **au**

☐ 29. J a n u a r y

☐ 30. l a n g u a g e   ☐ 43. **a u** n t

       ☐ 44. l **a u** g h

ACTIVITY 12 **Matching Common Words and Pictures**

Use the list in Activity 11 to write the common word that matches the picture.

1. _apple_ _____   3. _____

2. _____   4. _____

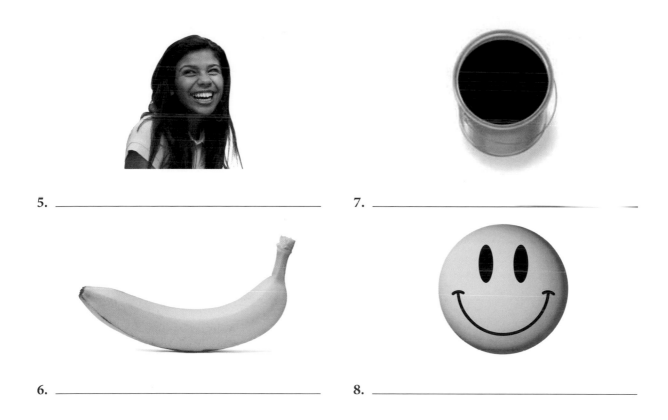

5. _____

7. _____

6. _____

8. _____

ACTIVITY 13   **Spelling Words with the Sound of a in cat**

Fill in the missing letters to spell words with the sound of **a** in c**a**t. Then copy the correct word.

1. m __ p   _____

2. l __ nguages   _____

3. __ fter   _____

4. h __ ppen   _____

5. b __ d   _____

6. h __ ve   _____

7. __ nd   _____

8. th __ t   _____

9. __ nimal   _____

10. fl __ g   _____

ACTIVITY 14   **Writing Sentences with Vocabulary in Context**

Complete each sentence with the correct word from Activity 13. Then copy the sentence with correct capital letters and end punctuation.

1. my cat is black ....**and**............ white

   My cat is black and white.

   _____

2. a cat is an ....

   _____

3. the students .... a question

   _____

4. my math class is .... lunch

   _____

5. that is a .... of the world

_____

6. what .... can you speak

_____

7. the .... of the United States is red, white, and blue

_____

8. something bad can .... at any time

_____

9. this apple is ....

_____

10. .... glass has a little tea in it

_____

ACTIVITY 15 **Scrambled Letters**

Change the order of the letters to write a word that has the sound of **a** in c**a**t.

_____ 1. e h v a

_____ 2. a k s

_____ 3. v e l r a t

_____ 4. a n d h

_____ 5. g u a g e l a n

_____ 6. t a

_____ 7. p e p a l

_____ 8. n k a t h

_____ 9. a p e n h p

_____ 10. c k a b

_____ 11. c k l a b

_____ 12. p a m

_____ 13. d n a

_____ 14. a t t h

CD 1,
Track 2  **ACTIVITY 16** **Spelling Practice**

Write the word that you hear. You will hear each word two times.

1. _____
2. _____
3. _____
4. _____
5. _____

6. _____
7. _____
8. _____
9. _____
10. _____

11. _____
12. _____
13. _____
14. _____
15. _____

ACTIVITY 17 Spelling Review: Which Word Is Correct?

This review covers the different ways of spelling the sound of **a** in c**a**t in this unit. Read each pair of words. Circle the word that is spelled correctly.

	A	B		A	B
1.	answr	answer	11.	aple	apple
2.	black	bleck	12.	aed	add
3.	klass	class	13.	after	aftr
4.	famili	family	14.	animal	animil
5.	fest	fast	15.	examble	example
6.	happen	heppen	16.	hand	hend
7.	saled	salad	17.	hav	have
8.	travl	travel	18.	thank	thanke
9.	aunt	aent	19.	lagh	laugh
10.	last	laest	20.	ask	ausk

For more practice with the **spelling and vocabulary** in this unit, go to NGL.Cengage.com/GWF.

Original Student Writing

Writing Your Ideas in Sentences

Write five to ten sentences on your own paper. Write about you and your family. For help, you can follow the examples in Activity 3 (page 7) and Activity 9 (page 11).

Peer Editing

Exchange papers from the above activity. Read your partner's sentences.
Then use Peer Editing Sheet 1 to make comments about the writing. Go to NGL.Cengage.com/GWF. There is a sample in Appendix 3.

For more practice with the **writing** in this unit, go to NGL.Cengage.com/GWF.

Nouns

Students walk near Villafranca del Bierzo,
Castilla y León, Spain.

OBJECTIVES **Grammar:** To learn about nouns
Vocabulary and Spelling: To study common words with the sound of <u>e</u> in b<u>e</u>d
Writing: To write about your classmates or friends

Can you write about your classmates or friends?

Grammar for Writing

person: **Sam**

place: **Mexico**

thing: **a lemon**

What Is a Noun?

✓ A **noun** is the name of a person, place, or thing.

person	a **boy**	a **girl**	my **teacher**	Joe	Ellen	Mrs. Lopez
place	a **city**	our **country**	a **hotel**	Paris	Mexico	Central Hotel
thing	a **language**	a **watch**	a **bed**	a **leg**	Honda	Pepsi

ACTIVITY 1 Finding Nouns in Sentences

Circle the 21 nouns in these sentences. The number in parentheses ( ) is the number of nouns in each sentence.

My Favorite Food

1. What is your favorite food? (1)

2. This is an excellent question. (1)

3. My favorite food for breakfast is a sandwich with eggs. (4)

4. My favorite food for lunch is salad. (3)

5. My favorite food for dinner is chicken with lemons and red peppers. (5)

6. My favorite food for dessert is chocolate. (3)

7. Chocolate is the best food. (2)

8. I like to eat chocolate after dinner. (2)

Singular or Plural?

✓ For one of a noun, you use the singular form.

✓ For two or more of a noun, you use the plural form. The plural usually ends in –s.

Singular	Plural	Spelling Rule
one **animal**	three **animal<u>s</u>**	add **–s**
one **address**	two **address<u>es</u>**	add **–es** after **–ch, –sh, –ss, –o, –x**
one **baby**	five **bab<u>ies</u>**	change **–y** to **–i** after a consonant and then add **–es**
one **day**	ten **day<u>s</u>**	do not change **–y** to **–i** after a vowel (**a, e, i, o, u**)
one **knife**	four **kni<u>ves</u>**	change **–f** to **–v** and then add **–es**

✓ Some nouns do not add **–s**. These **irregular nouns** have a different plural form.

man ➔ **men**	woman ➔ **women**	child ➔ **children**	mouse ➔ **mice**
foot ➔ **feet**	tooth ➔ **teeth**	fish ➔ **fish**	person ➔ **people**

✓ If you cannot count the noun, it has no plural form.

Noncount Nouns	Count Nouns
homework, furniture, water, bread	a **test**, a **salad**, a **glass** (of water), a **slice** (of bread)

ACTIVITY 2 · Writing Sentences with Correct Plurals

Copy the sentences. Use correct plurals for nouns. Remember to begin a sentence with a capital letter and use correct end punctuation.

1. two week have fourteen day

   Two weeks have fourteen days.

2. many young child have problem with their tooth

   _____

3. my teacher in my three morning class are three man from different country

   _____

4. next year my sister Anna and Emily want to visit Europe

   _____

5. how many day are there in a year

   _____

Proper Nouns

✓ A **proper noun** is the name of a specific person, place, or thing. Examples are names of people, places, days, months, languages, book titles, companies, rivers, and other specific nouns.

✓ A **proper noun** always begins with a capital letter.

✓ Do not use capital letters in the middle of a word or at the end of a word.

Noun	Proper Noun
a **city**	**Cairo**
a **teacher**	**Mr. Nelson**
days	**Friday** and **Saturday**
languages	**Spanish** and **Chinese**

Common Student Mistakes

Student Mistake X	Problem	Correct Example ✓
new york	capital letters missing at the beginning	**N**ew **Y**ork
emm**A**	capital letter missing at the beginning; capital letter at the end	**Emm**a
S**EPTEMBER**	all capital letters	**S**eptember
furniture**s**	noncount nouns are never plural	**furniture**
many famil**ys**	plural spelling	many famil**ies**

ACTIVITY 3 Finding Capital Letters in Nouns

Circle the 22 capital letters in these nouns. When you finish, count the letters to make sure there are 22 circles.

	Category	Examples			
1.	a city	Ⓓenver	New York	Paris	Athens
2.	food	a sandwich	a cake	a vegetable	pasta
3.	a month	January	February	March	April
4.	a country	Yemen	Saudi Arabia	Germany	Brazil
5.	a person	my aunt	Uncle Jack	my doctor	Dr. Benson
6.	a color	green	red	black	yellow
7.	a language	Spanish	English	Japanese	French

ACTIVITY 4 Capitalizing Proper Nouns

Copy these nouns. Use capital letters correctly.

1. paris _____

2. arabic _____

3. january _____

4. california _____

5. ben _____

6. emma _____

7. toyota _____

8. rolex _____

9. nile _____

10. pepsi _____

11. french _____

12. bangkok _____

ACTIVITY 5 Writing Answers with Nouns

Use the nouns from Activity 4 to answer these questions. Write complete sentences. Be careful with capital letters.

1. Which word is the first month of the year?

   January is the first month of the year.

2. Which word is a city in France?

   _____

3. Which word is a name for a boy?

   _____

4. Which word is a name for a girl?

   _____

5. Which word is a company that makes cars?

   _____

6. Which word is the language in Egypt and Morocco?

   _____

7. Which word is a company that makes very expensive watches?

   _____

8. Which word is a state in the United States?

   _____

ACTIVITY 6 Scrambled Letters

Use the letters to write the word next to the information. Be careful with capital letters.

Scrambled Letters	Helpful Information	Correct Word
e e e m b d r c	the last month of the year	1.
n v e e s	the number after six	2.
l l o y e w	a color	3.
r e p u	a country in South America	4.
m a k r d e n	a country in Europe	5.
w d s d a y e n e	a day of the week	6.
l n o m e	a yellow fruit	7.
s e y	the opposite of no	8.

ACTIVITY 7 Writing Definition Sentences with is

Write eight sentences with the information in Activity 6. Practice using the word **is**. Be careful with capital letters and periods.

1. _December is the last month of the year._

2. _____

3. _____

4. _____

5. _____

6. _____

7. _____

8. _____

ACTIVITY 8 Scrambled Sentences

Change the order of the words to write a correct sentence. Be careful with spelling, capital letters, punctuation, and word order.

My Story

1. my name amina is

_____

2. from senegal i am

_____

3. africa senegal is country in west a

_____

4. common name for amina is a girls in my country

_____

5. many country can understand two people in more than my languages

_____

6. french speak wolof and i can

_____

7. i english can also understand

_____

ACTIVITY 9 **Finding and Correcting 10 Mistakes**

Circle the ten mistakes. Then write the sentences correctly. The number in parentheses ( ) is the number of mistakes in that sentence. Be ready to explain your answers.

<	**May 2014**	>

Sun	Mon	Tue	Wed	Thu	Fri	Sat
				1	2	3
4	5	6	7	8	9	10
11	12	13	14	15	16	17
18	19	20	21	22	23	24
25	26	27	28	29	30	31

The Months of the Year

1. January is the first Month. (1)

_____

2. december Is the last Month. (3)

_____

3. december has 31 Days. (2)

_____

4. September has 30 day (2)

_____

5. My Favorite months is November. (2)

_____

CD 1,
Track 3  **ACTIVITY 10** **Dictation**

You will hear six sentences three times. Listen carefully and write the six sentences. The number in parentheses ( ) is the number of words in the sentence. Be careful with capital letters and end punctuation.

1. _____ (4)

2. _____ (6)

3. _____ (3)

4. _____ (5)

5. _____ (6)

6. _____ (5)

ACTIVITY 11 **Practicing Grammar and Vocabulary in Model Writing**

Read the sentences in the paragraph very carefully. Fill in the missing words from the word bank. Circle the 22 letters that need to be capital letters. Then copy the paragraph on your own paper.

photo	united	is	a lot
capital	country	from	hoyoung

The Excellent People in My Math Class

1 this is a _____ of my math class. **2** kyoko _____ from japan.

3 ahmad and mohamad are from the _____ arab emirates. **4** the united arab emirates

is a small _____ in the middle east. **5** _____ is from seoul. **6** seoul is

the _____ of korea. **7** carlos is _____ costa rica. **8** i like the men and

women in this class _____.

ACTIVITY 12 **Guided Writing: Making Changes in Model Writing**

Write the paragraph from Activity 11 again, but make the changes listed below. Sometimes you will have to make other changes, too.

Sentence 1. Change **photo** to **picture**. Then change **math** to **English.**

Sentence 3. Add **two men** in the correct place.

Sentence 4. Change **the United Arab Emirates** to **Saudi Arabia**. Then change **small** to **large.**

Sentence 7. Add **a young man** in the correct place.

Sentence 8. Change **men and women** to **students.**

_____

_____

_____

_____

_____

_____

_____

_____

For more practice with the **grammar** in this unit, go to NGL.Cengage.com/GWF.

Building Vocabulary and Spelling

Learning Words with the Sound of e in bed*

e = b **e** d   This sound is usually spelled with the letters **e, ea,** and others.

b e d

h e a d

ACTIVITY 13 **Which Words Do You Know?**

This list has 47 words with the sound of **e** in b**e**d.

1. Notice the spelling patterns.

2. Check the words you know.

3. Look up new words in a dictionary. Write the meanings in your Vocabulary Notebook.

Common Words

GROUP 1:
Words spelled with **e**

☐ 1. b e d
☐ 2. b e s t
☐ 3. c h e c k
☐ 4. e g g
☐ 5. e n d
☐ 6. e n t e r
☐ 7. e v e r y

☐ 8. e x e r c i s e
☐ 9. g e t
☐ 10. h e l l o
☐ 11. h e l p
☐ 12. l e f t
☐ 13. l e g
☐ 14. l e t

*List is from: Spelling Vocabulary List © 2013 Keith Folse

☐ 15. m e n

☐ 16. n e c e s s a r y

☐ 17. n e v e r

☐ 18. n e x t

☐ 19. p e n

☐ 20. p e t

☐ 21. r e d

☐ 22. s e l l

☐ 23. s e v e n

☐ 24. s p e l l

☐ 25. t e l l

☐ 26. t e n

☐ 27. t e s t

☐ 28. t e x t

☐ 29. w e l l

☐ 30. w e n t

☐ 31. w e s t

☐ 32. w h e n

☐ 33. y e l l o w

☐ 34. y e s

GROUP 2:
Words spelled with **ea**

☐ 35. a l r e a d y

☐ 36. b r e a d

☐ 37. b r e a k f a s t

☐ 38. d e a d

☐ 39. h e a d

☐ 40. r e a d y

☐ 41. w e a t h e r

GROUP 3:
Other spellings

☐ 42. a g a i n

☐ 43. a n y

☐ 44. f r i e n d

☐ 45. m a n y

☐ 46. s a i d

☐ 47. s a y s

ACTIVITY 14 **Matching Common Words and Pictures**

Use the list in Activity 13 to write the common word that matches the picture.

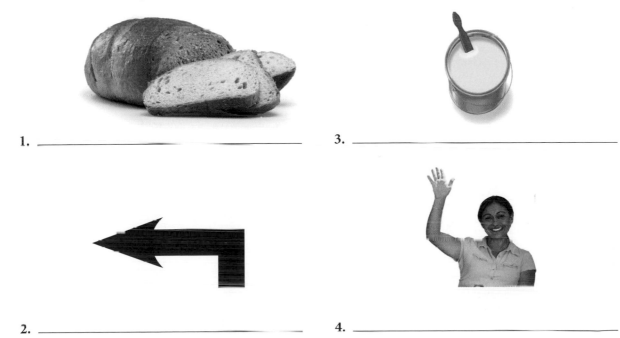

1. _____

3. _____

2. _____

4. _____

5. _____   7. _____

6. _____   8. _____

ACTIVITY 15 **Spelling Words with the Sound of e in bed**

Fill in the missing letters to spell words with the sound of **e** in b**e**d. Then copy the correct word.

1. br __ d   _____   7. g __ t   _____

2. d __ d   _____   8. n __ ver   _____

3. t __ st   _____   9. wh __ n   _____

4. b __ st   _____   10. s __ s   _____

5. m __ ny   _____   11. r __ dy   _____

6. w __ ll   _____   12. p __ t   _____

ACTIVITY 16 **Writing Sentences with Vocabulary in Context**

Complete each sentence with the correct word from Activity 15. Then copy the sentence with correct capital letters and end punctuation.

1. my .... is a black and white cat

   _____

2. .... is your birthday

   _____

3. .... people live in china and india

   _____

4. I go to the bank to .... some cash

_____

5. anna and emily are my .... friends

_____

6. my car battery is ....

_____

7. you can make a good sandwich with meat and ....

_____

8. my brother and I .... eat meat

_____

9. susan can speak english very ....

_____

10. my best friend always .... hello to everyone

_____

11. are you .... to eat dinner now

_____

12. we have a big spelling .... tomorrow

_____

ACTIVITY 17 **Scrambled Letters**

Change the order of the letters to write a word that has the sound of **e** in b**e**d.

_____ **1.** l l e w   _____ **8.** p e l l s

_____ **2.** r e w a t h e   _____ **9.** l e t l

_____ **3.** n e t x   _____ **10.** a a i g n

_____ **4.** f r n d e i   _____ **11.** e m n

_____ **5.** w c l l o y   _____ **12.** d e r

_____ **6.** e l p h   _____ **13.** n t w e

_____ **7.** c k c h e   _____ **14.** a d h e

ACTIVITY 18 **Spelling Practice**

Write the word that you hear. You will hear each word two times.

1. _____   6. _____   11. _____

2. _____   7. _____   12. _____

3. _____   8. _____   13. _____

4. _____   9. _____   14. _____

5. _____   10. _____   15. _____

ACTIVITY 19 **Spelling Review: Which Word Is Correct?**

This review covers the different ways of spelling the sound of <u>e</u> in b<u>e</u>d in this unit. Read each pair of words. Circle the word that is spelled correctly.

	A	B		A	B
1.	wether	weather	11.	seven	sevn
2.	wint	went	12.	alredy	already
3.	bed	baid	13.	any	eny
4.	ready	raidy	14.	bred	bread
5.	sais	says	15.	dead	ded
6.	heallo	hello	16.	weall	well
7.	many	meny	17.	tel	tell
8.	agein	again	18.	test	tst
9.	breakfast	brekfast	19.	spll	spell
10.	friend	frend	20.	eagg	egg

ACTIVITY 20 **Cumulative Spelling Review**

Read the four words in each row from Units 1 and 2. Underline the word that is spelled correctly.

	A	B	C	D
1.	lenguage	language	langage	languege
2.	naver	nevr	never	neaver
3.	happan	hapen	happen	hapan

	A	B	C	D
4.	neaxt	nxt	naxt	next
5.	rdey	rcdy	rady	ready
6.	weathr	wether	weather	wather
7.	heavy	hvy	havy	hevy
8.	meny	menie	many	mny
9.	sayed	said	sead	sede
10.	agan	egain	agean	again
11.	friend	frnd	frend	freand
12.	brekfast	briekfast	breakfast	brkfast
13.	travl	traval	treval	travel
14.	efter	eafter	after	aufter
15.	inter	enter	cntra	etrin
16.	cnswcr	eanswer	acnswer	answer
17.	laff	lauff	lagh	laugh
18.	wint	went	wnt	weint

For more practice with the **spelling and vocabulary** in this unit, go to NGL.Cengage.com/GWF.

Original Student Writing

Writing Your Ideas in Sentences or a Paragraph

Write five to ten sentences on your own paper. Write about your classmates or friends. Tell their names and the country or city where they are from. For help, you can follow the examples in Activity 11 (page 26) and Activity 12 (page 27). (For more information about writing a paragraph, go to Appendix 4.)

Peer Editing

Exchange papers from the above activity. Read your partner's sentences.
Then use Peer Editing Sheet 2 to make comments about the writing. Go to NGL.Cengage.com/GWF.
There is a sample in Appendix 3.

For more practice with the **writing** in this unit, go to NGL.Cengage.com/GWF.

Verbs: Simple Present Tense

Three monks hold a lantern at the Yi Peng sky lantern festival in Chiang Mai, Thailand.

OBJECTIVES Grammar: To learn about simple present tense
Vocabulary and Spelling: To study common words with the sound of <u>i</u> in f<u>i</u>sh
Writing: To write about things that people usually do

*Can you write about
things that people
usually do?*

Grammar for Writing

I **wake up** early.

I **eat** bread and jam for breakfast.

I **go** (to school) by bus.

What Is a Verb?

✓ A **verb** is a word that shows action (or existence).

> I **teach** English every day.
>
> I **am** a teacher at Wilson College.
>
> I **drive** to school at 7:30 a.m.
>
> I **arrive** at school at 8:00 a.m.
>
> My first class **begins** at 8:30 a.m.
>
> It **is** a writing class.

✓ The tense of the verb usually tells the time of the action. (The Brief Writer's Handbook explains tenses.)

Simple Present Tense

✓ **Simple present tense** is used for actions that happen many times or are always true. (See Brief Writer's Handbook for other verb tenses.)

✓ Common time expressions for simple present tense include **always, never,** and **every.**

✓ In simple present tense, each verb has two forms: **live, lives.**

20 Common Verbs You Need to Know*	
1. am	I **am** from the United States.
2. are	Your answers **are** excellent.
3. come	We never **come** home late.
4. find	Can you **find** my country on that map?
5. get	I **get** many e-mails every day.

*Based on the General Service List, Corpus of Contemporary American English, and other corpus sources

6. **give**	The teacher **gives** a test to every student.	
7. **go**	You **go** to school by car.	
8. **has**	My name **has** ten letters.	
9. **have**	We **have** many friends.	
10. **is**	Everything **is** OK.	
11. **know**	You **know** French and Spanish.	
12. **like**	She **likes** coffee with milk and sugar.	
13. **look**	Please **look** at question number ten.	
14. **make**	I **make** coffee every morning.	
15. **say**	Please **say** your name slowly.	
16. **see**	I **see** you.	
17. **take**	Please **take** a cookie.	
18. **think**	I **think** the time is seven o'clock.	
19. **use**	I **use** my cell phone many times every day.	
20. **work**	He **works** at the bank.	

ACTIVITY 1   Finding Verbs in Sentences

Circle the ten verbs in these sentences. Each sentence has one verb.

My Mondays

1. Monday (is) a difficult day for me.

2. My day begins very early.

3. I take a shower at 6 a.m.

4. I drink a cup of coffee with milk and sugar.

5. I eat a light breakfast.

6. I usually eat toast with jam.

7. Sometimes I eat cereal with milk.

8. Then I go to school.

9. I have five classes on Monday.

10. I am usually tired after school.

Read the sentences. Then fill in the missing verbs from the word bank. Write the sentences with a capital letter and a period.

make	eat	fly	run
swim	jump	are	sit

Talking about Animals

1. giraffes .... leaves

_____

2. penguins .... black and white

_____

3. fish .... in the ocean

_____

4. horses .... very fast

_____

5. monkeys .... in trees

_____

6. birds .... in the sky

_____

7. bees .... honey

_____

8. frogs .... over rocks and plants

_____

Two Verb Forms of Simple Present Tense: -s and no -s

✓ In simple present tense, verbs have two forms.

Simple Form*	speak, write, do	the verb as in the dictionary with no endings (no –s, no –ed, no –ing)
The –s or –es Form**	speaks, writes, does	the verb + –s or –es

*base form or dictionary form
** 3rd person singular

✓ For verbs with **I, you, we,** and **they,** use the dictionary form.

✓ For verbs with **he, she,** and **it,** use the form that ends in –s.

	make	know	think
Singular	I **make**	I **know**	I **think**
	you **make**	you **know**	you **think**
	he **makes**	he **knows**	he **thinks**
	she **makes**	she **knows**	she **thinks**
	it **makes**	it **knows**	it **thinks**
Plural	we **make**	we **know**	we **think**
	you **make**	you **know**	you **think**
	they **make**	they **know**	they **think**

✓ For verbs that end in –o, –ch, –sh, –ss, and –x, add –es.

–o	–ch	–sh	–ss	–x
I **go**	we **watch**	you **wash**	I **guess**	they **mix**
she **goes**	he **watches**	it **washes**	he **guesses**	she **mixes**

Spelling Verbs with –es

Write the correct form of the verb with each subject.

1. teach	**2.** finish	**3.** pass	**4.** do
you *teach*	he	I	it
she *teaches*	we	the bus	children

5. miss	**6.** catch	**7.** go	**8.** push
you	he	my plane	you
she	we	people	he

✓ English has 26 letters: 5 vowels (**a, e, i, o, u**) and 21 consonants.
  • For verbs that end in a consonant + **y**, change the –**y** to –**i** and add –**es**.
  • For verbs that end in a vowel + **y**, add –**s**.

consonant + y		vowel + y	
I **try**	they **cry**	I **say**	we **play**
she **tries**	the baby **cries**	he **says**	the boy **plays**

Spelling Verbs with –s or –ies

Write the correct form of the verb with each subject.

1. study	**2.** carry	**3.** buy	**4.** stay
we	she	they	we
she	you	the doctor	my uncle

5. hurry	**6.** try	**7.** fly	**8.** enjoy
you	a student	pilots	every child
she	students	a pilot	children

Irregular Verbs in Simple Past Tense

✓ The verbs **be** and **have** are irregular. You must memorize the forms of these verbs.

	be	have
singular	I **am**	I **have**
	you **are**	you **have**
	he **is**	he **has**
	she **is**	she **has**
	it **is**	it **has**
Plural	we **are**	we **have**
	you **are**	you **have**
	they **are**	they **have**

Common Student Mistakes

Student Mistake X	Problem	Correct Example ✓
Ed and **Linda in** Texas.	verb missing	Ed and Linda **live** in Texas.
Ed **work** in a big office.	**–s** ending missing	Ed work**s** in a big office.
Ed **is wakes up** at 6 a.m. every day.	extra verb	Ed **wakes up** at 6 a.m. every day.
Ed **trys** to sleep seven hours every night.	spelling of the verb	Ed tr**ies** to sleep seven hours every night.

ACTIVITY 5 Writing Verbs in Sentences

Read the sentences about one man's job. Then fill in the missing words from the word bank.

takes	eats	watches	is	takes
drives	puts	wakes	begins	listens

A Taxi Driver

1. Ahmed _____ a taxi driver.

2. He _____ a taxi from 8 a.m. to 4 p.m. five days a week.

3. He _____ up at 6:30 a.m.

4. He _____ his day with a cup of black coffee.

5. He _____ a quick shower.

6. Ahmed _____ on a pair of pants and a nice shirt.

7. Then he _____ something for breakfast.

8. Sometimes he _____ the morning news on TV.

9. Ahmed _____ to news on the radio in his taxi.

10. He _____ customers to many different places.

ACTIVITY 6 Writing Complete Sentences

Circle the verb in each sentence. Then copy the sentences. Use capital letters and periods.

My Class

1. i (study) english at smith college

    I study English at Smith College.

2. my english is not so good

3. i am in the beginning class

4. my class has 12 students

5. i am from saudi arabia

6. four students come from japan

7. they speak japanese

_____

8. five students speak spanish

_____

9. they come from mexico and peru

_____

10. meilin is from china

_____

11. she speaks chinese

_____

12. one student comes from korea

_____

13. his name is kwan

_____

14. i like all the students in my class very much

_____

Negative of Verbs in Simple Present Tense

Making a negative is very easy. You use a special helping verb—**do** or **does**—before the word **not**.

✓ Use **do not** + verb after **I, you, we** or **they**.

✓ Use **does not** + verb after **he, she,** or **it**.

	have	know	do
Singular	I **do not** have	I **do not** know	I **do not** do
	you **do not** have	you **do not** know	you **do not** do
	he **does not** have	he **does not** know	he **does not** do
	she **does not** have	she **does not** know	she **does not** do
	it **does not** have	it **does not** know	it **does not** do
Plural	we **do not** have	we **do not** know	we **do not** do
	you **do not** have	you **do not** know	you **do not** do
	they **do not** have	they **do not** know	they **do not** do

✓ You can also use a short form: **doesn't, don't**. This is called a **contraction**. It is used in speaking and in friendly writing such as e-mail. Do not use contractions in formal writing.

Full Form	I **do not** have a problem. He **does not** know the answer. It **does not** make any difference.	Use in academic writing (or in very formal speaking).
Contraction	I **don't** have a problem. He **doesn't** know the answer. It **doesn't** make any difference.	Use in e-mail and friendly writing (or in conversation).

Common Student Mistakes

Student Mistake X	Problem	Correct Example ✓
Ed and Linda **no live** in Korea.	wrong negative	Ed and Linda **do not live** in Korea.
Ed **do not works** in a big office.	–s ending on verb	Ed **does not work** in a big office.
Ed **is not** wake up at 7 a.m. every day.	wrong verb with **not**	Ed **does not** wake up at 7 a.m. every day.

ACTIVITY 7 **Writing Negative Sentences**

The information about these countries is not correct. Write the sentences again. Use negative verbs. Be careful with capital letters and periods.

Information about Seven Countries

1. people in brazil speak spanish

    People in Brazil do not speak Spanish.

2. the flag of colombia has four colors

3. most people in canada work on sunday

4. the capital of japan is kyoto

5. most people in saudi arabia work on friday

6. drivers in dubai drive on the left side of the street

7. the flag of the united states has five colors

_____

8. people in japan speak chinese

_____

Scrambled Sentences

Change the order of the words to write a correct sentence. Be careful with spelling, capital letters, punctuation, and word order.

Jason Thompson's Job

1. very jason a job thompson important has

_____

2. he of president a is the company

_____

3. he company every goes to his day

_____

4. to the company he seven gets at

_____

5. leaves at six he

_____

6. not go does home early he

_____

7. talks with many he people

_____

8. free he lot of does not have a time

_____

9. happy very he is his job at

_____

Circle the ten mistakes. Then write the sentences correctly. The number in parentheses ( ) is the number of mistakes in that sentence. Be ready to explain your answers.

Our New Year's Celebration in Mexico

1. I am from mexico. (1)

_____

2. My favorit holiday is New Year's. (1)

_____

3. We celebrate it at Midnight on December 31. (1)

_____

4. We are eat 12 grapes in one minute. (1)

_____

5. We eat one grapes for each month of the year. (1)

_____

6. We make a wish for 12 good thing for the new year. (1)

_____

7. My famili and I eat a really big dinner together. (1)

_____

8. Sometimes we eat Turkey. (1)

_____

9. Sometimes we eats a special Mexican food called mole. (1)

_____

10. My family and I not leave our house on this important day. (1)

_____

ACTIVITY 10 Dictation

You will hear six sentences three times. Listen carefully and write the six sentences. The number in parentheses ( ) is the number of words in the sentence. Be careful with capital letters and end punctuation.

1. _____ (7)

2. _____ (6)

3. _____ (8)

4. _____ (5)

5. _____ (6)

6. _____ (5)

ACTIVITY 11 Practicing Grammar and Vocabulary in Model Writing

Read the sentences in the paragraph very carefully. Fill in the missing words from the word bank. Circle the fourteen letters that need to be capital letters. Then copy the paragraph on your own paper.

always	lincoln	call	play	and
breakfast	every	they	are	at

Twin Sisters

1 laura _____ maria are students. **2** _____ like school very much. **3** they go to _____ high school. **4** they eat breakfast _____ 7:00 a.m. **5** they enjoy _____ very much. **6** they _____ eat eggs and bread for breakfast. **7** sometimes they _____ their friends after breakfast. **8** they _____ good students. **9** _____ night they study for an exam. **10** sometimes they _____ video games on the computer.

47

Write the paragraph from Activity 11 again, but make the changes listed below. Sometimes you will have to make other changes, too.

<u>Sentence 1</u>. Change **Laura and Maria** to **Maria**. Then make changes in the other sentences. Be careful with subject–verb agreement.

<u>Sentence 4</u>. Change the time to any other reasonable time to eat breakfast.

<u>Sentence 7</u>. Change **call** to **text**.

<u>Sentence 8</u>. Change **good** to **excellent**.

<u>Sentence 9</u>. Change **night** to **weekend**.

_____

_____

_____

_____

_____

_____

_____

_____

For more practice with the **grammar** in this unit, go to NGL.Cengage.com/GWF.

Building Vocabulary and Spelling

Learning Words with the Sound of i in fish *

i = f**i**s h   This sound is usually spelled with the letter **i** and others.

fish

bridge

Activity 13   **Which Words Do You Know?**

This list has 45 words with the sound of **i** in fi**sh**.

1. Notice the spelling patterns.

2. Check ✓ the words you know.

3. Look up new words in a dictionary. Write the meanings in your Vocabulary Notebook.

Common Words

GROUP 1:
Words spelled with **i**

☐ 1. b i g

☐ 2. b r i d g e

☐ 3. c h i c k e n

☐ 4. c i t y

☐ 5. d e l i c i o u s

☐ 6. d i d

☐ 7. d i f f e r e n t

☐ 8. d i f f i c u l t

☐ 9. d i n n e r

☐ 10. d r i n k**

☐ 11. f i s h

☐ 12. g i v e

☐ 13. h i m

☐ 14. h i s

☐ 15. i f

☐ 16. i n

☐ 17. i n t e r e s t i n g

☐ 18. i s

☐ 19. i t

☐ 20. k i t c h e n

*List is from: Spelling Vocabulary List © 2013 Keith Folse
Note: The vowel in the letters –ink** (e.g., in the word **drink**) may sound like the **e** in **he** or **eat** to some speakers.

☐ 21. l i s t	☐ 35. t h i n k*
☐ 22. l i t t l e	☐ 36. t h i s
☐ 23. l i v e	☐ 37. w h i c h
☐ 24. m i l k	☐ 38. w i l l
☐ 25. m i n u t e	☐ 39. w i n
☐ 26. p i n k*	☐ 40. w i n t e r
☐ 27. r i n g	☐ 41. w i t h
☐ 28. s i c k	
☐ 29. s i n g	**GROUP 2:**
☐ 30. s i s t e r	Other spellings
☐ 31. s i t	☐ 42. p r e t t y
☐ 32. s i x	☐ 43. b e e n
☐ 33. s w i m	☐ 44. w o m e n
☐ 34. t h i n g	☐ 45. b u s y

*Note: The vowel in the letters –ink (e.g., in the words **pink** and **think**) may sound like the **e** in he or **eat** to some speakers.

ACTIVITY 14 **Matching Words and Pictures**

Use the list in Activity 13 to write the common word that matches the picture.

1. _____

3. _____

2. _____

4. _____

5. _____

7. _____

6. _____

8. _____

ACTIVITY 15 **Spelling Words with the Sound of i̱ in fi̱sh.**

Fill in the missing letters to spell words with the sound of **i̱** in fi̱sh. Then copy the correct word.

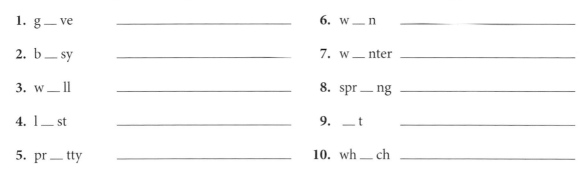

1. g __ ve _____

2. b __ sy _____

3. w __ ll _____

4. l __ st _____

5. pr __ tty _____

6. w __ n _____

7. w __ nter _____

8. spr __ ng _____

9. __ t _____

10. wh __ ch _____

ACTIVITY 16 Writing Sentences with Vocabulary in Context

Complete each sentence with the correct word from Activity 15. Then copy the sentence with correct capital letters and end punctuation.

1. .... car do you like

_____

2. can you .... me a different book

_____

3. i want to .... the football match tomorrow

_____

4. all the plants are green in ....

_____

5. the weather can be very cold in ....

_____

6. here is a .... of things we need for dinner

_____

7. everybody in our office is so .... today

_____

8. we .... take a big exam tomorrow

_____

9. those roses are really ....

_____

10. my english class has eight men and ten .... in it

_____

ACTIVITY 17 Scrambled Letters

Change the order of the letters to write a word that has the sound of **i** in f**i**sh.

_____ **1.** s b y u

_____ **2.** i c h w h

_____ **3.** s s t r e i

_____ **4.** i n k d r

_____ **5.** p t y r e t

_____ **6.** e t u i m n

_____ **7.** d d l e i m

_____ **8.** g t h i n

_____ **9.** e g i v

_____ **10.** b e n e

_____ **11.** m n o e w

_____ **12.** e n k t i c h

ACTIVITY 18 Spelling Practice

Write the word that you hear. You will hear each word two times.

1. _____   6. _____   11. _____

2. _____   7. _____   12. _____

3. _____   8. _____   13. _____

4. _____   9. _____   14. _____

5. _____   10. _____   15. _____

ACTIVITY 19 Spelling Review: Which Word Is Correct?

This review covers the different ways of spelling the sound of **i** in f**i**sh in this unit. Read each pair of words. Circle the word that is spelled correctly.

	A	B		A	B
1.	chicken	checkin	11.	sing	seng
2.	did	ded	12.	sitt	sit
3.	pritty	pretty	13.	thnk	think
4.	ben	been	14.	hes	his
5.	giv	give	15.	intrsting	interesting
6.	if	ife	16.	little	littl
7.	list	listc	17.	dennir	dinner
8.	city	sity	18.	swime	swim
9.	big	bigg	19.	bisy	busy
10.	liv	live	20.	women	womin

ACTIVITY 20 **Cumulative Spelling Review**

Read the four words in each row from Units 1–3. Underline the word that is spelled correctly.

	A	B	C	D
1.	denner	dinnr	denner	dinner
2.	limun	limon	lemon	lemin
3.	esimple	simple	semble	semple
4.	frind	frend	freind	friend
5.	bein	been	bn	ben
6.	everything	evrithing	everythng	evrithng
7.	swem	eswem	eswim	swim
8.	niver	nivr	never	nivr
9.	happan	hapen	happen	happin
10.	bisy	busy	buesy	bissy
11.	neaxt	nixt	nxt	next
12.	minute	menit	minit	menute
13.	pik	pick	bik	bick
14.	egain	agen	again	agin
15.	ridy	redy	rady	ready
16.	letle	littl	little	litl
17.	winter	wnter	wintir	wentir
18.	enstead	instead	ensted	insted
19.	Jenuary	January	Jinuary	Jonuary
20.	laugh	leagh	lagh	laf

💻 For more practice with the **spelling and vocabulary** in this unit, go to NGL.Cengage.com/GWF.

Original Student Writing

Writing Your Ideas in Sentences or a Paragraph

Write five to ten sentences on your own paper. Write about things that people usually do. Use simple present tense. For help, you can follow the examples in Activity 11 (page 47) for one person or Activity 12 (page 48) for two or more people. (For more information about writing a paragraph, go to Appendix 4.)

Peer Editing

Exchange papers from the above activity. Read your partner's sentences.
Then use Peer Editing Sheet 3 to make comments about the writing. Go to NGL.Cengage.com/GWF. There is a sample in Appendix 3.

For more practice with the **writing** in this unit, go to NGL.Cengage.com/GWF.

Adjectives

Fishermen on Inle Lake in Myanmar take their
boats out on a beautiful morning.

OBJECTIVES **Grammar:** To learn about adjectives
Vocabulary and Spelling: To study common words with the sound of <u>o</u> in h<u>o</u>t
Writing: To write about places around the world

*Can you describe
a place you know?*

Grammar for Writing

This **big** bridge is in the United States.

This **long** bridge is in China.

What Is an Adjective?

✓ An **adjective** is a word that describes a noun or a pronoun.

✓ There are different types of adjectives. They all give information about a person, a place, or a thing.

✓ When an adjective and a noun are together, the adjective comes first.

Type of Adjective	Adjectives	Examples in Sentences
Descriptive Adjectives	black, happy, bad, big, hot, difficult, pretty, empty, ready	**Black** clouds mean **bad** weather. Learning English is **difficult**.
Possessive Adjectives	my, your, his, her, its, our, their	**My** car is next to **your** house.
Demonstrative Adjectives	this, that, these, those	**Those** students need **these** pens.
Quantity Adjectives	some, six, ten, many, three	**Many** students have **three** classes.
Nouns Working as Adjectives	all nouns	My **math** exam is difficult. Mr. Miller works in a **pet** store.
Articles*	a, an, the	**A** book is on **the** table.

*You will find more information about articles in Unit 8.

Descriptive Adjectives

✓ **Descriptive adjectives** describe a noun or a pronoun.

✓ Descriptive adjectives come **before a noun** or **after the verb <u>be</u>** (am, is, are).

✓ There is no difference in the form of the adjective for a singular noun or a plural noun.

Singular		Plural	
before a noun:	We have a <u>**new** clock</u>.	before a noun:	We have two <u>**new** clocks</u>.
after **be:**	Our clock **is** <u>**new**</u>.	after **be:**	Our two clocks **are** <u>**new**</u>.

20 Common Descriptive Adjectives You Need to Know*

1. another	I have **another** exam tomorrow.	
2. bad	The weather is very **bad** today.	
3. big	They live in a **big** house.	
4. different	Arabic and Korean are **different** languages.	
5. early	I have an **early** class on Monday and Wednesday.	
6. first	My **first** class begins at 8 a.m.	
7. good	This pizza is very **good**.	
8. great	Mona is a **great** friend.	
9. high	People do not like **high** prices.	
10. important	This information is **important** to me.	
11. last	The **last** bus is at 9 p.m.	
12. late	I am always **late** for class.	
13. little	A **little** cat is a kitten.	
14. long	Going from London to Sydney is a **long** trip.	
15. new	Do you have a **new** bed?	
16. next	We are going there **next** Saturday.	
17. old	My grandmother is very **old**.	
18. right	What is the **right** answer to question 5?	
19. same	You and I have the **same** birthday.	
20. young	Michael is a nice **young** man.	

Based on the General Service List, Corpus of Contemporary American English, and other corpus sources

Common Endings for Descriptive Adjectives

Many adjectives have a special ending. Three very common endings for adjectives are **–y, –ful,** and **–ous**. This list has 32 adjectives with adjective endings. You probably know some of these adjectives already.

Endings	Descriptive Adjectives with –y, –ful, and –ous Endings
–y	angr**y** craz**y** eas**y** funn**y** health**y** hungr**y** rain**y** salt**y** sleep**y** sunn**y** bus**y** dirt**y** empt**y** happ**y** heav**y** laz**y** read**y** scar**y** spic**y** thirst**y**
–ful	beauti**ful** care**ful** color**ful** help**ful** use**ful** wonder**ful**
–ous	danger**ous** delici**ous** fam**ous** jeal**ous** nerv**ous** previ**ous**

Common Student Mistakes

Student Mistake X	Problem	Correct Example ✓
I have a **car red**.	word order	I have a **red car**.
She has ten **reds** apples.	plural adjective	She has ten **red** apples.

ACTIVITY 1 **Finding Descriptive Adjectives**

These sentences have examples of the 52 descriptive adjectives on page 59. Read the sentences. Then circle the descriptive adjectives in each sentence. The number in parentheses ( ) is the number of descriptive adjectives in that sentence.

1. Your mother is angry about your dirty room. (2)

2. The young girl with a colorful sweater is very sleepy now. (3)

3. Our first names have the same spelling. (2)

4. This spicy pizza is so delicious. (2)

5. Rainy weather makes many people feel sleepy or lazy. (3)

6. High prices for food are very bad for everyone. (2)

7. My old classroom is empty now. (2)

8. The new soccer team from Spain is wonderful. (2)

ACTIVITY 2 **Writing Two Sentences with Descriptive Adjectives**

Write two sentences with the same descriptive adjective. In the first sentence, put the descriptive adjective before the noun. In the second sentence, use a possessive adjective and the verb **be** (**am, is, are**) to write a new sentence. Be careful with word order.

1. **green**   I have a book.

   before a noun: _I have a green book._

   after **be**:   _My book is green._

2. **good**   They speak English.

   before a noun: _____

   after **be**:   _____

3. **fast**   You have a car.

   before a noun: _____

   after **be**:   _____

4. **good**   She speaks Spanish.

   before a noun: _____

   after **be**: _____

5. **big**   My father works in an office.

   before a noun: _____

   after **be**: _____

6. **new**   My sister has a job.

   before a noun: _____

   after **be**: _____

7. **interesting**   My father and my sister have pets.

   before a noun: _____

   after **be**: _____

8. **little**   We live in a house.

   before a noun: _____

   after **be**: _____

Possessive Adjectives

✓ **Possessive adjectives** tell you the owner. These adjectives are:
   my   your   his   her   its   our   their
   They come in front of a noun.

✓ There is no difference in the form of the adjective for a singular noun or a plural noun.
   my book, my books

Singular Noun	Plural Noun
subject: **I** have a book. possessive: It is **my** book.	subject: **We** have books. possessive: **Our** books are black.
subject: **You** have a car. possessive: **Your** car is white.	subject: **You** have cars. possessive: Where are **your** cars?
subject: **He** has a watch. possessive: It is **his** watch.	subject: **They** have watches. possessive: **Their** watches are new.
subject: **She** has a bag. possessive: **Her** bag is black.	subject: **They** have bags. possessive: Which are **their** bags?

Common Student Mistakes

Student Mistake X	Problem	Correct Example ✓
Mary has **his** phone.*	wrong possessive adjective	Mary has **her** phone.
They have **theirs** laptops.	plural spelling	They have **their** laptops.
I do not have **me** book.	form of adjective	I do not have **my** book.

*This sentence is possible, but it means Mary has John's phone, not her phone.

Using Possessive Adjectives in Connected Sentences

Complete the sentences with the correct possessive adjectives.

1. John Smith is from the United States. _____ passport is dark blue.

2. Ahmed Al-Turki is from Saudi Arabia. _____ passport is green.

3. Elena Vestri is from Italy. _____ passport is red.

4. My good friend Mei is from China. _____ passport is green.

5. My classmate Gustavo is from Brazil. _____ passport is blue.

6. My sister and I are from Turkey. _____ passports are dark red.

7. Manuel and Gerardo Ramirez are from Mexico. _____ passports are very dark green.

8. Mona is from the United Arab Emirates. _____ passport is dark blue.

9. Kyoko and _____ brother have passports from Japan. _____ passports are red.

10. Enrique and _____ sister have passports from Ecuador. _____ passports are dark red.

ACTIVITY 4 **Using Subjects and Possessive Adjectives in Longer Writing**

Complete the sentences with the correct subjects or possessive adjectives. Be careful with capital letters.

1. Susan likes rings. _____ has many pretty rings. _____ favorite ring is from Turkey.

2. Abdul is from Saudi Arabia. _____ passport is green. _____ speaks Arabic. _____ lives with _____ family in Jeddah.

3. Maria is from Peru. _____ speaks Spanish. _____ works at a big bank. _____ likes _____ job very much. _____ job is not difficult.

4. Maria and Pedro Martinez have two children. _____ children are in high school. _____ are excellent students. _____ son is in 10th grade. _____ name is José. _____ is very hard-working. _____ daughter is in 9th grade. _____ name is Tina. _____ is very smart. _____ is very good at math.

Demonstrative Adjectives

✓ The **Demonstrative adjectives** are:
   this, that, these, those
   They come in front of a noun.

✓ **This** and **that** are singular. **These** and **those** are plural.

Meaning	Singular	Plural
near the speaker	**This** passport is blue.	**These** passports are blue.
not near the speaker	**That** passport is red.	**Those** passports are red.

Common Student Mistakes

Student Mistake X	Problem	Correct Example ✓
These lesson is simple.	plural adjective	**This** lesson is simple.
Are very good these books.	word order	**These** books are very good.

ACTIVITY 5 Using <u>this</u>, <u>that</u>, <u>these</u>, and <u>those</u> in Sentences

Underline the correct demonstrative adjective in each sentence.

1. I can't answer (this, these) exam questions.

2. (That, Those) glass is empty.

3. Who is (this, that) man over there?

4. (This, These) English students are from Colombia.

5. Can you help me with (this, these) question?

6. (This, These) map is the best for your class.

7. The teacher can explain (that, those) grammar lesson again.

8. (That, Those) eggs are for your breakfast tomorrow.

9. Are (that, those) spelling words very difficult?

10. Do you know (that, those) women?

11. (This, These) apple drink is delicious.

12. I really like (this, these) rings a lot.

Nouns Working as Adjectives

✓ **Nouns** can also work as **adjectives** in a sentence. The noun that works as an adjective comes in front of the second noun.

✓ Nouns working as adjectives cannot be plural. Remember that adjectives do not change for singular or plural.

Example of noun (as adjective) + noun	Meaning
my **Tuesday** class	The class is on Tuesday.
a **math** test	The test is about math.
a **tomato** salad	The salad has tomatoes in it.
a **pet** store	The store sells pets.

ACTIVITY 6 Practicing Writing Nouns as Adjectives

Write the first sentence again, but put information from the second sentence in the first sentence. Then write your new sentence. Be careful with word order and adjective form (no plural).

1. Please make a salad. Put tomatoes in the salad.

    Please make a tomato salad.

2. My teacher can answer this question. The question is about math.

    _____

3. These forks are good. The fork is made of plastic.

    _____

4. Please call me on Tuesday. Call me in the afternoon.

    _____

5. I need some shoes. The shoes are for tennis.

    _____

6. I walk to the station every morning. The station is for buses.

    _____

7. This is a book. The book is about rocks.

    _____

8. Let's meet at the shop. The shop sells coffee.

    _____

9. We have an exam tomorrow. The exam is for practice.

    _____

10. Please come to the meeting. The meeting is in the morning.

_____

11. Their garden is big. The garden has vegetables.

_____

12. Their garden is pretty. The garden has flowers.

_____

ACTIVITY 7 **Scrambled Sentences**

Change the order of the words to write a correct sentence. Sometimes more than one answer is possible. Be careful with capitalization, end punctuation, and word order.

1. two yellow cats black on that are taxi

_____

2. tomato salad is this delicious

_____

3. two has big houses our family

_____

4. my three difficult can big sister understand languages

_____

5. like this jim really lemon and his friends drink

_____

6. languages people in many speak two morocco

_____

7. your is difficult last name

_____

8. has three his watch new hands

_____

9. chinese and the red yellow flag is

_____

10. for lettuce those please use fresh salads

_____

ACTIVITY 8 Finding and Correcting 10 Mistakes

Circle the ten mistakes. Then write the sentences correctly. The number in parentheses ( ) is the number of mistakes in that sentence. Be ready to explain your answers.

The UAE

1. The UAE mean the United Arab Emirates. (1)

   _____

2. The UAE is a countrys on the persian Gulf. (2)

   _____

3. The UAE has seven emirate. (1)

   _____

4. These emirates Abu Dhabi, Ajman, Dubai, Fujairah, Ras al-Khaimah, Sharjah, and Umm al-Quwain. (1)

   _____

5. The capital are Abu Dhabi. (1)

_____

6. Two countries very near the UAE have Oman and Saudi Arabia. (1)

_____

7. The UAE flag have four color. (2)

_____

8. People from the UAE is Emiratis. (1)

_____

  **ACTIVITY 9** **Dictation**

You will hear six sentences three times. Listen carefully and write the six sentences. The number in parentheses ( ) is the number of words in the sentence. Be careful with capital letters and end punctuation.

1. _____ (5)

2. _____ (6)

3. _____ (7)

4. _____ (5)

5. _____ (9)

6. _____ (8)

Read the sentences in the paragraph very carefully. Fill in the missing words from the word bank. Circle the 27 letters that need to be capital letters. Then copy the paragraph on your own paper.

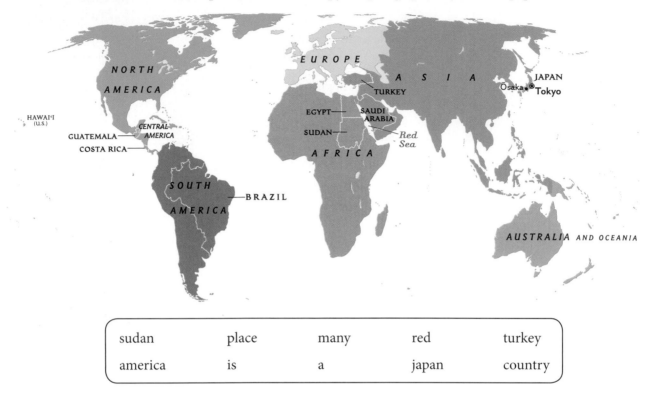

| sudan | place | many | red | turkey |
| america | is | a | japan | country |

Finding Cities and Countries on a World Map

1 here we see a large map with _____ places. **2** tokyo is a large city in

_____ . **3** osaka is _____ large city in japan. **4** costa rica is a country

in central _____ . **5** guatemala is a _____ in central america.

6 the _____ sea is between saudi arabia and egypt. **7** brazil _____

a country in south america. **8** _____ is a country in africa. **9** a part of

_____ is in europe. **10** australia is a very beautiful _____ .

ACTIVITY 11 Guided Writing: Making Changes in Model Writing

Write the paragraph from Activity 10 again, but make the changes listed below. Sometimes you will have to make other changes, too.

Sentence 1. Change **large** to **colorful**. Add **interesting** to describe **places.**

Sentences 2 and 3. Combine these two sentences. Begin the new sentence with **Tokyo and Osaka …**

Sentences 4 and 5. Combine these two sentences. Begin the new sentence with **Costa Rica and Guatemala …**

Sentences 4 and 5. Add **beautiful** in the correct place.

Sentence 6. Change the order of the countries.

Sentence 7. Add **very big** in the correct place.

Sentence 8. Add **big** in the correct place.

Sentence 9. Add **small** in the correct place.

Sentence 10. Change **very beautiful** to **interesting.**

_____

_____

_____

_____

_____

_____

_____

_____

_____

_____

For more practice with the **grammar** in this unit, go to NGL.Cengage.com/GWF.

ACTIVITY 14 **Spelling Words with the Sound of o in hot**

Fill in the missing letters to spell words with the sound of **o** in h**o**t. Then copy the correct word.

1. j __ b   _____

2. imp __ ssible   _____

3. d __ ctor   _____

4. b __ x   _____

5. g __ t   _____

6. p __ t   _____

7. l __ t   _____

8. c __ mmon   _____

9. h __ t   _____

10. n __ t   _____

ACTIVITY 15 **Writing Sentences with Vocabulary in Context**

Complete each sentence with the correct word from Activity 14. Then copy the sentence with correct capital letters and end punctuation.

1. the weather in Miami in july is very …………

_____

2. what is your ………… at the company

_____

3. smith and jones are very ………… last names in england

_____

4. this beautiful ………… of chocolates is from your friend

_____

5. his last name is ………… smith

_____

6. there is a ………… of soup on the stove for the children

_____

7. sick people go to see their …………

_____

8. yesterday i ………… a special letter from the bank

_____

9. a ………… of students in my class have expensive cell phones

_____

10. a purple cat is …………

_____

ACTIVITY 16 Scrambled Letters

Change the order of the letters to write a word that has the sound of <u>o</u> in h<u>o</u>t.

_____ 1. o G d   _____ 6. b o r

_____ 2. y d o b   _____ 7. o c k r

_____ 3. o p t   _____ 8. h e r f a t

_____ 4. p h s o   _____ 9. o c l k

_____ 5. c n m o o m   _____ 10. o c l k c

CD 1, Track 8

ACTIVITY 17 Spelling Practice

Write the word that you hear. You will hear each word two times.

1. _____   6. _____   11. _____

2. _____   7. _____   12. _____

3. _____   8. _____   13. _____

4. _____   9. _____   14. _____

5. _____   10. _____   15. _____

ACTIVITY 18 Spelling Review: Which Word Is Correct?

This review covers the different ways of spelling the sound of <u>o</u> in h<u>o</u>t in this unit. Read each pair of words. Circle the word that is spelled correctly.

	A	B		A	B
1.	everybady	everybody	11.	drop	drap
2.	fother	father	12.	got	gott
3.	bottle	botle	13.	lot	lat
4.	God	Gad	14.	October	Octaber
5.	imposible	impossible	15.	possible	posible
6.	bodi	body	16.	shap	shop
7.	botom	bottom	17.	soks	socks
8.	bax	box	18.	sombody	somebody
9.	clok	clock	19.	common	comon
10.	coton	cotton	20.	hot	het

Read the four words in each row from Units 1–4. Underline the word that is spelled correctly.

	A	B	C	D
1.	bax	box	becks	bocks
2.	limun	limon	lemon	lemun
3.	stop	stap	estop	estap
4.	cammen	cammon	commen	common
5.	frund	frind	frend	friend
6.	rab	rob	rabb	robb
7.	everything	evrithing	everythng	evrithng
8.	sokz	soks	socks	saks
9.	niver	nivor	never	nover
10.	hoppan	hapen	happen	hoppen
11.	drep	drop	drap	drahp
12.	botm	batm	bottom	botom
13.	minit	minute	menit	menute
14.	klok	klock	clok	clock
15.	agin	agen	again	agein
16.	ready	ridy	redy	rady
17.	letle	littl	little	lottle
18.	buzy	busy	bisi	bizi
19.	enstead	insted	instead	ensted
20.	Oktobr	Oktober	October	Octobr

🖥 For more practice with the **spelling and vocabulary** in this unit, go to NGL.Cengage.com/GWF.

Original Student Writing

Writing Your Ideas in Sentences or a Paragraph

Write five to ten sentences on your own paper. Write about places in the world, such as cities, states, countries, or any places you want. Use adjectives in your sentences. For help, you can follow the examples in Activity 10 (page 68) and Activity 11 (page 69). (For more information about writing a paragraph, go to Appendix 4.)

Peer Editing

Exchange papers from the above activity. Read your partner's sentences.
Then use Peer Editing Sheet 4 to make comments about the writing. Go to NGL.Cengage.com/GWF. There is a sample in Appendix 3.

For more practice with the **writing** in this unit, go to NGL.Cengage.com/GWF.

Verbs: Simple Present Tense of *be*

Saint Basil's Cathedral is in Red Square, Moscow.

Can you write about two cities?

Grammar for Writing

My cousin **is** from Russia.

The Verb **be**

✓ The verb **be** has three forms in the simple present tense: **am, is, are.**

✓ There is no difference in the form of the subject **you** for one person (singular) or **you** for many people (plural).

be	
Singular	**Plural**
I **am**	we **are**
you **are**	you **are**
Dave **is**	Dave and Mary **are**
Mary **is**	Mary and Dave **are**
my house **is**	our houses **are**

ACTIVITY 1 **Writing Sentences with <u>be</u>: Where Are They from?**

Write sentences to tell where these people are from. Use country names in your sentences.

1.

2.

3.

4.

Linda – England   Wei – China   Marcos – Brazil   Toshio – Japan

| 5. | 6. | 7. | 8. |
| Atsuro – Japan | Claire – England | Faisal – Saudi Arabia | Maria – Guatemala |

1. (Linda) __Linda is from England.__

2. (Wei) _____

3. (Marcos) _____

4. (Toshio) _____

5. (Toshio and Atsuro) _____

6. (Linda and Claire) _____

7. (Faisal) _____

8. (Maria) _____

ACTIVITY 2 **Writing Sentences with _be_: Where Are You from?**

What does each person write? Look at the picture in Activity 1. Write two sentences with the name of the person and his or her country.

1. Wei writes: __My name is Wei. I am from China.__

2. Marcos writes: _____

3. Linda and Claire write: _____

_____

4. Faisal writes: _____

5. Toshio writes: _____

6. Atsuro and Toshio write: _____

_____

7. Maria writes: _____

8. Linda writes: _____

Negative of <u>be</u> in Simple Present Tense

✓ Making a negative with **be** is very easy. You add **not** after **am, is,** and **are**.

✓ Add **not** for a negative: **am not, is not, are not**.

✓ You can also use a short form (called a **contraction**) in speaking and in friendly writing such as e-mail: **isn't, aren't**. Do not use contractions in formal writing.

Negative of <u>be</u> in Simple Present Tense	
Singular	**Plural**
I **am** <u>**not**</u>	we **are** <u>**not**</u> we <u>**aren't**</u>
you **are** <u>**not**</u> you <u>**aren't**</u>	you **are** <u>**not**</u> you <u>**aren't**</u>
Dave **is** <u>**not**</u> Dave <u>**isn't**</u> Mary **is** <u>**not**</u> Mary <u>**isn't**</u> my house **is** <u>**not**</u> my house <u>**isn't**</u>	Dave and Mary **are** <u>**not**</u> they **are** <u>**not**</u> Dave and Mary <u>**aren't**</u> they <u>**aren't**</u>

ACTIVITY 3 Writing Sentences with Correct Information

These sentences have wrong information. Write two negative sentences with the same meaning. Then write one positive sentence to give correct information. Follow the examples.

1. Tokyo is in China.
   a. _Tokyo is not in China._
   b. _Tokyo isn't in China._
   c. _Tokyo is in Japan._

2. New York is a small city.
   a. _New York is not a small city._
   b. _New York isn't a small city._
   c. _New York is a very big city._

3. Pizza and sushi are from Greece.
   a. _____
   b. _____
   c. _____

4. Mexico is three hundred years old.

    a. _____

    b. _____

    c. _____

5. I am five years old.

    a. _____

    b. _____

    c. _____

6. Today is January 1.

    a. _____

    b. _____

    c. _____

7. A gold ring is a cheap gift.

    a. _____

    b. _____

    c. _____

8. You are a famous singer.

    a. _____

    b. _____

    c. _____

Simple Present Tense Sentences with <u>be</u>

✓ What comes after **be**? Sentences with **am, is,** and **are** can have different endings.

Subject + <u>am</u> <u>is</u> <u>are</u>	Second Part of the Sentence	Type of Information
a. I **am**	a **student**.	noun
b. I **am**	**smart**.	adjective
c. I **am**	a **smart student**.	adjective + noun
d. You **are**	**in California.**	place
e. My meeting **is**	**at 11 o'clock.**	time

Scrambled Sentences

Change the order of the words to write a correct sentence. Then tell what kind of information is in the second part of the sentence by writing the letter **a, b, c, d,** or **e** from the chart on page 81.

1. cook a mother my is good

   <u>My mother is a good cook.</u>   <u>c</u>

2. are from my cousins california

   _____   _____

3. are swimmers my best not excellent friends

   _____   _____

4. our next to india trip is month

   _____   _____

5. the math the table books are on

   _____   _____

6. michael on and rob are vacation

   _____   _____

7. about questions are math our easy

   _____   _____

8. football are sports and tennis

   _____   _____

Common Student Mistakes

Student Mistake X	Problem	Correct Example ✓
<u>Mary a</u> good person.	verb missing	Mary **is** a good person.
The boys **is** in the kitchen.	singular verb with plural subject	The boys **are** in the kitchen.
That computer **no is** expensive.	wrong negative	That computer **is not** expensive.

Scrambled Sentences with <u>be</u>

Change the order of the words to write a correct sentence. Sometimes more than one answer is possible. Be careful with capitalization, end punctuation, and word order.

1. not is a my math brother teacher

   _____

2. sofia and emily aren't from san diego

_____

3. my with james meeting currier is 9 at o'clock

_____

4. brazil not são paolo is the capital of

_____

5. very city in large vancouver is a canada

_____

6. vegetable a a tomato not is

_____

7. the colors of yellow and red the chinese are flag

_____

8. these not are very watches expensive

_____

ACTIVITY 6 **Finding and Correcting 10 Mistakes**

Circle the ten mistakes. Then write the sentences correctly. The number in parentheses ( ) is the number of mistakes in that sentence. Be ready to explain your answers.

Ecuador

1. Ecuador is a country beautiful in South America. (1)

_____

2. The name Ecuador is means equator. (1)

_____

3. About fifteen million people lives in Ecuador. (1)

_____

4. Three big city in Ecuador are Guayquil, Quito, and Cuenca. (1)

_____

5. Many tourists comes to Ecuador each years. (2)

_____

6. This tourists come to see the beautifuls mountains. (2)

_____

7. These tourists also come to see the animals interesting on the galapagos Islands. (2)

_____

CD 1, Track 9  **ACTIVITY 7** **Dictation**

You will hear six sentences three times. Listen carefully and write the six sentences. The number in parentheses ( ) is the number of words in the sentence. Be careful with capital letters and end punctuation.

1. _____ (5)

2. _____ (6)

3. _____ (7)

4. _____ (5)

5. _____ (7)

6. _____ (8)

ACTIVITY 8 **Practicing Grammar and Vocabulary in Model Writing**

Read the sentences in the paragraph very carefully. Fill in the missing words from the word bank. Circle the 22 letters that need to be capital letters. Then copy the paragraph on your own paper.

jeddah	the	here	weather
riyadh	are	is	saudi

A Lesson about Saudi Arabia

1 _____ we see a map of the middle east. **2** our lesson today is about _____ arabia. **3** jeddah and _____ are two cities in saudi arabia. **4** _____ is a very important city. **5** jeddah _____ not the capital of saudi arabia. **6** _____ capital of saudi arabia is riyadh. **7** the people in jeddah _____ very nice. **8** the _____ in jeddah is hot in the summer.

ACTIVITY 9 **Guided Writing: Making Changes in Model Writing**

Write the paragraph from Activity 8 again, but make the changes listed below and all other necessary changes.

Sentence 1. Change **the Middle East** to **North America**. Add **colorful** to describe **map.**

Sentence 2. Change **Saudi Arabia** to **the United States** here and other places, where necessary.

Sentence 3. Change **Jeddah** to **New York** and **Riyadh** to **Washington, D.C.** here and other places, where necessary.

Sentence 8. Write information about the weather in the winter.

_____

_____

_____

_____

_____

_____

_____

_____

_____

_____

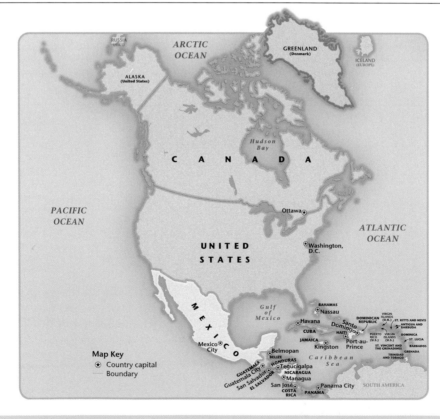

For more practice with the **grammar** in this unit, go to NGL.Cengage.com/GWF.

Building Vocabulary and Spelling

Learning Words with the Sound of u in cup*

u = c **u** p This sound is usually spelled with the letters **u, o, a, ou, tion** or **sion,** and others.

c u p   s o f a

K o r e a

ACTIVITY 10 **Which Words Do You Know?**

This list has 55 common words with the sound of **u** in c**u**p.

1. Notice the spelling patterns.

2. Check ✓ the words you know.

3. Look up new words in a dictionary. Write the meanings in your Vocabulary Notebook.

Common Words

GROUP 1:
Words spelled with **u**

☐ 1. b u s
☐ 2. c u p
☐ 3. c u t
☐ 4. f u n
☐ 5. f u n n y
☐ 6. h u s b a n d
☐ 7. j u l y
☐ 8. j u s t

☐ 9. l u n c h
☐ 10. m u s t
☐ 11. n u m b e r
☐ 12. r u n
☐ 13. s u m m e r
☐ 14. s u n
☐ 15. S u n d a y
☐ 16. u n d e r
☐ 17. u p

*List is from: Spelling Vocabulary List © 2013 Keith Folse

GROUP 2:

Words spelled with **o**

- [ ] 18. b r o t h e r
- [ ] 19. c o m e
- [ ] 20. c o m p a n y
- [ ] 21. c o m p u t e r
- [ ] 22. K o r e a
- [ ] 23. M o n d a y
- [ ] 24. m o n e y
- [ ] 25. m o n t h
- [ ] 26. m o t h e r
- [ ] 27. n o n e
- [ ] 28. o n e
- [ ] 29. o t h e r
- [ ] 30. s o n
- [ ] 31. t o d a y
- [ ] 32. t o g e t h e r

GROUP 3:

Words spelled with **a**

- [ ] 33. a b o u t
- [ ] 34. a b o v e
- [ ] 35. A m e r i c a
- [ ] 36. a n o t h e r
- [ ] 37. B r a z i l
- [ ] 38. J a p a n

- [ ] 39. s o f a
- [ ] 40. w a n t
- [ ] 41. w a s
- [ ] 42. w h a t

GROUP 4:

Words spelled with **ou**

- [ ] 43. c o u n t r y
- [ ] 44. c o u s i n
- [ ] 45. e n o u g h
- [ ] 46. f a m o u s
- [ ] 47. t r o u b l e
- [ ] 48. y o u n g

GROUP 5:

Words ending in **–tion** or **–sion**

- [ ] 49. a c t i o n
- [ ] 50. d i s c u s s i o n
- [ ] 51. q u e s t i o n

GROUP 6:

Other spellings

- [ ] 52. b e c a u s e
- [ ] 53. b e f o r e
- [ ] 54. P e r u
- [ ] 55. d o e s

Use the list in Activity 10 to write the common word that matches the picture.

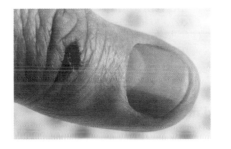

1. _____

2. _____

1   2   9   7
10 15 22 33

?

3. _____

6. _____

4. _____

7. _____

5. _____

8. _____

Read the four words in each row from Units 1–5. Underline the word that is spelled correctly.

	A	B	C	D
1.	truble	trable	troble	trouble
2.	famos	femous	famous	femous
3.	posible	possbli	passeble	possible
4.	uncle	ancile	oncle	unkil
5.	onion	onien	onin	oniun
6.	frenly	frendly	friendly	freindly
7.	family	famely	famly	fomly
8.	lenguaje	languaje	language	lenguage
9.	summer	sumer	sammer	samer
10.	defficult	difficult	deficalt	difficalt
11.	Ingles	Inglish	Englishe	English
12.	everybody	everybady	evrybody	evrybady
13.	very	bery	wery	bary
14.	busines	bisiness	business	bisiness
15.	come	com	cume	coume
16.	cuestion	question	kwestion	cuoustion
17.	beacos	becos	because	becuse
18.	socs	socks	sockes	saucks
19.	necesari	necessari	necesary	necessary
20.	cntinue	continue	cuntinue	countinue

For more practice with the **spelling and vocabulary** in this unit, go to NGL.Cengage.com/GWF.

Original Student Writing

Writing Your Ideas in Sentences or a Paragraph

Write five to ten sentences on your own paper. Write about two cities in the same country. Use a large city and the capital city from the same country. Choose from the list below or choose two other cities you know about (but one must be the capital).

For help, you can follow the examples in Activity 8 (page 85) or Activity 9 (page 86). You can use the Internet for information, but do not copy sentences from the Internet. Use your own original writing. (For more information about writing a paragraph, go to Appendix 4.)

Canada:	Montreal	Ottawa	**Ecuador:**	Guayaquil	Quito
Turkey:	Istanbul	Ankara	**China:**	Shanghai	Beijing
Japan:	Osaka	Tokyo	**Peru:**	Arequipa	Lima
Italy:	Milan	Rome	**Korea:**	Pusan	Seoul
United States:	San Diego	Washington D.C.	**Brazil:**	Rio de Janeiro	Brasilia
Saudi Arabia:	Jeddah	Riyadh	**Columbia:**	Medellin	Bogota

Peer Editing

Exchange papers from the above activity. Read your partner's sentences.

Then use Peer Editing Sheet 5 to make comments about the writing. Go to NGL.Cengage.com/GWF. There is a sample in Appendix 3.

For more practice with the **writing** in this unit, go to NGL.Cengage.com/GWF.

Pronouns

A veterinarian cleans the teeth of a hippopotamus at the zoo in Medellín, Colombia.

OBJECTIVES **Grammar:** To learn about pronouns
Vocabulary and Spelling: To study common words with the sound of **a** in **cake**
Writing: To write about people and their jobs

Can you write about people and their jobs?

Grammar for Writing

Here is a photo of my mother, my grandmother, and my sisters. **They** are always happy.

This is my family's house. We like **it** a lot.

What Is a Pronoun?

✓ A **pronoun** is a word that can take the place of a noun.

✓ Two common types of pronouns are **subject pronouns** and **object pronouns**.

Placement of Pronouns	
Subject Pronouns	**Object Pronouns**
I see the cat.	The cat sees **me.**
You see the cat.	The cat sees **you.**
He sees the cat.	The cat sees **him.**
She sees the cat.	The cat sees **her.**
We see the cat.	The cat sees **us.**
You see the cat.	The cat sees **you.**
They see the cat.	The cat sees **them.**

ACTIVITY 1 **Finding Pronouns in Sentences**

Circle the 15 subject and object pronouns in these sentences.

1. My name is Robert. I am from Boston.

2. My sister calls me Bob. She likes Bob better than Robert.

3. She really likes the name Bob. I do not like it very much.

4. My sister is a teacher. We talk about her class sometimes.

5. She has 28 students in her class. She teaches math to them.

6. They like her class. It is very interesting.

What Is the Difference between Subject and Object Pronouns?

✓ A **subject pronoun** usually comes before the verb. It is the subject of the sentence.

    verb
    I <u>see</u> Mary.

✓ An **object pronoun** can come after a verb.

      verb
    Mary <u>sees</u> **him**.

✓ An **object pronoun** can also come after a preposition.

       preposition
    This pen is <u>for</u> **him**.

Types of Pronouns	Usual Places	Examples
subject pronoun	before the verb	**I** <u>see</u> the cat.
object pronoun	after the verb	The cat <u>sees</u> **me.**
	after a preposition	Our teacher explains ten new words <u>to</u> **us** every Monday.

ACTIVITY 2 Choosing the Correct Pronoun

Underline the correct pronoun in each sentence.

1. (I, Me) live with Joe and Mark. (They, Them) are nice people. It is easy to live with (they, them).

2. (I, Me) don't like tests. (They, Them) are very difficult for (I, me).

3. Can (you, your) explain these answers to (I, me) again? (I, Me) do not understand (it, them).

4. The president and his wife are very busy tonight. The president of Russia is in the United States now. (They, Them) have a special dinner for (he, him) tonight.

5. Most people in South America speak Spanish. People in Brazil do not speak Spanish. (They, Them) speak Portuguese. (He, She, It) is not the same as Spanish. (It, They) are different languages.

ACTIVITY 3 Writing Sentences with Subject and Object Pronouns

Read the first sentence. Then think of a second sentence that uses the words in parentheses and a pronoun. Write both sentences. Be careful with pronouns, capital letters, and end punctuation.

1. I like this shirt. (very nice)

   I like this shirt. It is very nice.

2. We want to eat some carrots. (we like)

   We want to eat some carrots. We like them.

3. Ellen and Ali work at the bank. (like their jobs)

   _____

4. You need to talk to Maria. (please call)

   _____

5. Where are my keys? (do you have)

   _____

6. Where are my keys? (aren't on the table)

   _____

7. My friends like chocolate. (this chocolate cake is for)

   _____

8. My friends like chocolate. (is delicious)

   _____

9. That computer is expensive. (you can't buy)

   _____

10. Lucas needs this check. (please take it to)

   _____

Common Student Mistakes

Student Mistake X	Problem	Correct Example ✓
Maria is my friend. **He** is nice	subject pronoun	Maria is my friend. **She** is nice.
Where are my keys? I can't find **it**.	object pronoun	Where are my keys? I can't find **them.**
My mother **she** is 42 years old.	noun + pronoun for the same person	**My mother** is 42 years old. Or: **She** is 42 years old.

ACTIVITY 4 **Practicing Pronouns, Capital Letters, and Periods**

Divide the line of words into two sentences. Write the sentences with correct capital letters and periods. Put one line under the subject pronouns. Put two lines under the object pronouns.

1. meilin is from china she speaks chinese

   Meilin is from China. <u>She</u> speaks Chinese.

2. our uncle wants to talk to my sister and me he needs to talk to us soon

3. my mother cooks pasta for my children she loves to cook it for them

4. my math class has twenty students in it they are from five countries

5. my friends and i play soccer every saturday we are pretty good at it

6. two of the students come from japan they are brothers

7. my cousin and i study english at smith college we really like it very much

8. carlos speaks spanish and english well they are easy for him

Change the order of the words to write a correct sentence. Be careful with spelling, capital letters, punctuation, and word order.

A Very Busy Doctor

1. maria gonzalez doctor is a

   _____

2. is doctor a she baby

   _____

3. about their come to babies see parents her

   _____

4. them helps problems with their she health

   _____

5. sometimes has more ten her office in people it than

   _____

6. want with the all to talk they doctor

   _____

7. busy is very always she

   _____

8. to see long wait her time families a

   _____

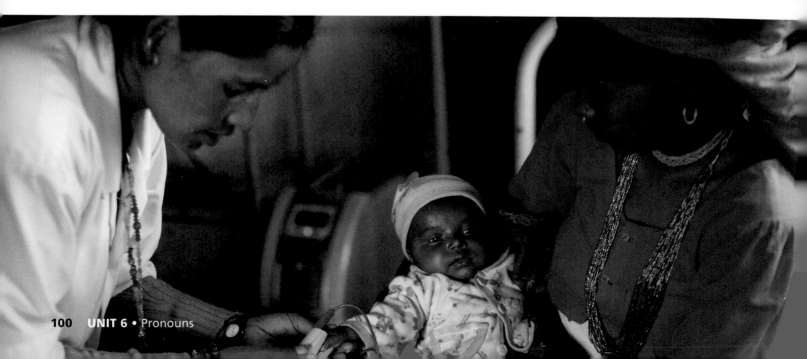

ACTIVITY 6 **Finding and Correcting 10 Mistakes**

Circle the ten mistakes. Then write the sentences correctly. The number in parentheses ( ) is the number of mistakes in that sentence. Be ready to explain your answers.

My Grandparents

1. My grandmother and my grandfather are people interesting. (1)

_____

2. My grandmother has 82 years old. (1)

_____

3. He is a cook wonderful. (2)

_____

4. My grandfather 80 years old. (1)

_____

5. She takes care of they garden and their pets. (2)

_____

6. My grandparents live in california. (1)

_____

7. Like their house very much. (1)

_____

8. We visit they about five or six times each year. (1)

_____

ACTIVITY 7 **Dictation**

You will hear six sentences three times. Listen carefully and write the six sentences. The number in parentheses ( ) is the number of words. Be careful with capital letters and end punctuation.

1. _____ (8)

2. _____ (6)

3. _____ (10)

4. _____ (5)

5. _____ (6)

6. _____ (10)

ACTIVITY 8 **Practicing Grammar and Vocabulary in Model Writing**

Read the sentences in the paragraph very carefully. Fill in the missing words from the word bank. Circle the 14 letters that need to be capital letters. Then copy the paragraph on your own paper.

his	it	these	some	martinez
you	he	officer	job	dangerous

My Cousin

1 _____ sentences are about my cousin. **2** his name is carlos

_____. **3** he is a police _____. **4** this _____

is very difficult. **5** this job is very _____. **6** _____ is at

work from 3 p.m. to 1 a.m. **7** _____ days off are sunday and monday.

8 _____ people like this kind of job. **9** i do not like _____.

10 what do _____ think about this job?

ACTIVITY 9 Guided Writing: Making Changes in Model Writing

Write the paragraph from Activity 8 again, but make the changes listed below and all other necessary changes.

Sentence 1. Change **cousin** to **cousins**. Then make changes to nouns, pronouns, and verbs where needed in the sentences. Be careful with singular and plural.

Sentence 2. Add **and Jose Garcia** in the correct place.

Sentences 4 and 5. Combine these two sentences into one sentence with seven words that begin **This job**.

Sentence 8. Add **a lot** in the correct place.

Sentence 9. Add **very much** in the correct place.

Sentence 10. Change **you** to **most people**.

For more practice with the **grammar** in this unit, go to NGL.Cengage.com/GWF.

Building Vocabulary and Spelling

Learning Words with the Sound of a in cake *

a = c **a** k **e**   This sound is usually spelled with the letters **a** + consonant + final **e**, **ai, ay, ea, ei,** and others.

c a k e

r a i n

ACTIVITY 10 Which Words Do You Know?

This list has 45 common words with the sound of **a** in c**a**k**e**. This sound is difficult because it can be spelled in many different ways.

1. Notice the spelling patterns.

2. Check ✔ the words you know.

3. Look up new words in a dictionary. Write the meanings in your Vocabulary Notebook.

Common Words

GROUP 1:
Words spelled with **a** + **consonant** + **final e**

- ☐ 1. a g e
- ☐ 2. a t e
- ☐ 3. c h a n g e
- ☐ 4. f a c e
- ☐ 5. g a m e
- ☐ 6. g a v e
- ☐ 7. g r a d e
- ☐ 8. l a t e

- ☐ 9. m a d e
- ☐ 10. m a k e
- ☐ 11. n a m e
- ☐ 12. p a g e
- ☐ 13. p l a c e
- ☐ 14. s a m e
- ☐ 15. s t a t e
- ☐ 16. t a b l e

- ☐ 17. t a k e
- ☐ 18. w a k e

GROUP 2:
Words spelled with **ai**

- ☐ 19. a f r a i d
- ☐ 20. e x p l a i n
- ☐ 21. f a i l
- ☐ 22. m a i l

*List is from: Spelling Vocabulary List © 2013 Keith Folse

☐ **23.** m a i n

☐ **24.** p a i d

☐ **25.** r a i n

☐ **26.** t r a i n

☐ **27.** w a i t

GROUP 3:
Words spelled with **ay** (usually at the end of a word)

☐ **28.** a l w a y s

☐ **29.** d a y

☐ **30.** h o l i d a y

☐ **31.** m a y be

☐ **32.** p a y

☐ **33.** p l a y

☐ **34.** p r a y

☐ **35.** s a y

☐ **36.** t o d a y

☐ **37.** w a y

☐ **38.** y e s t e r d a y

GROUP 4:
Words spelled with **ea** (in the middle of a word)

☐ **39.** b r e a k

☐ **40.** g r e a t

☐ **41.** s t e a k

GROUP 5:
Words spelled with **ei**

☐ **42.** e i g h t

☐ **43.** n e i g h b o r

GROUP 6:
Other spellings

☐ **44.** p a p e r

☐ **45.** t h e y

ACTIVITY 11 **Matching Words and Pictures**

Use the list in Activity 10 to write the common word that matches the picture.

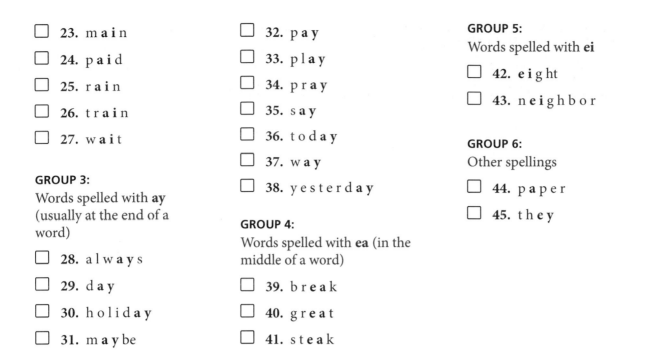

1. _____

3. _____

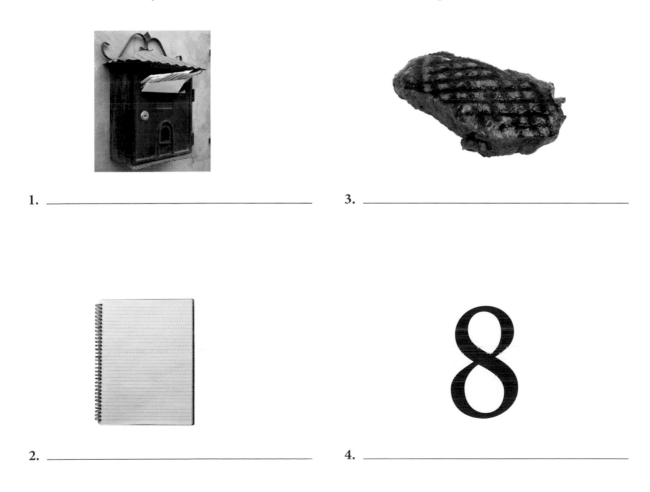

2. _____

4. _____

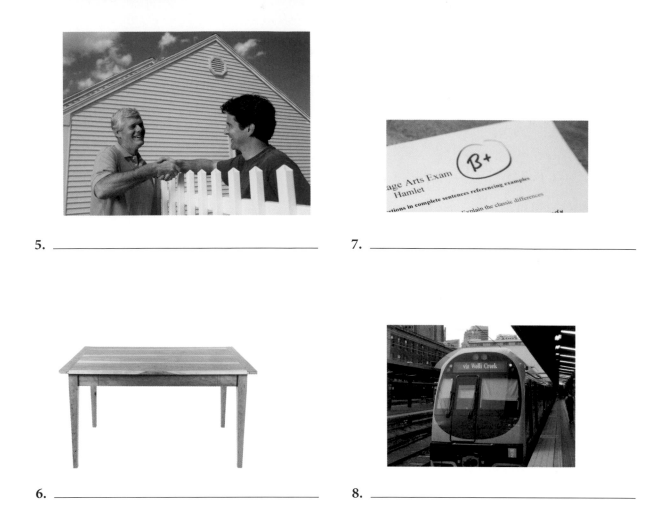

5. _____

7. _____

6. _____

8. _____

ACTIVITY 12 **Spelling Words with the Sound of <u>a</u> in c<u>a</u>k<u>e</u>**

Fill in the missing letters to spell words with the sound of <u>**a**</u> in c<u>**a**</u>k<u>**e**</u>. Then copy the correct word.

1. m __ be _____

2. pl __ c __ _____

3. tr __ n _____

4. w __ t _____

5. m __ d __ _____

6. __ t __ _____

7. n __ ghbor _____

8. afr __ d _____

9. m __ n _____

10. gr __ t _____

11. __ g __ _____

12. holid __ _____

13. m __ k __ _____

14. yesterd __ _____

ACTIVITY 13 Writing Sentences with Vocabulary in Context

Complete each sentence with the correct word from Activity 12. Then copy the sentence with correct capital letters and end punctuation.

1. london is an excellent ………… to visit

   _____

2. this rice dish with carrots and chicken is really …………

   _____

3. what is your cousin's …………

   _____

4. what is your favorite ………… of the year

   _____

5. ………… my friend and i went to the airport

   _____

6. every day i ………… a sandwich for lunch

   _____

7. we can go by bus or by …………

   _____

8. can you please ………… for me for just a minute

   _____

9. i am ………… of snakes

   _____

10. who ………… all of my chocolate cake

    _____

11. what is your ………… reason for studying english in canada instead of the united states

    _____

12. ………… it will rain on saturday

    _____

13. my aunt ………… chicken and rice for all of us

    _____

14. my ………… has a great house

    _____

ACTIVITY 14 Scrambled Letters

Change the order of the letters to write a word that has the sound of <u>a</u> in c<u>a</u>k<u>e</u>.

_____ 1. a k e t

_____ 2. m a s e

_____ 3. d t a y o

_____ 4. e g h i t

_____ 5. w a t i

_____ 6. d e a m

_____ 7. k a m e

_____ 8. g r e d a

_____ 9. s y a

_____ 10. m a e n

_____ 11. a y r p

_____ 12. s t t e a

_____ 13. y a w

_____ 14. d a y s r y t e e

CD 1, Track 12 ·))) ## ACTIVITY 15 Spelling Practice

Write the word that you hear. You will hear each word two times.

1. _____

2. _____

3. _____

4. _____

5. _____

6. _____

7. _____

8. _____

9. _____

10. _____

11. _____

12. _____

13. _____

14. _____

15. _____

ACTIVITY 16 **Spelling Review: Which Word Is Correct?**

This review covers the different ways of spelling the sound of **a** in c**a**k**e** in this unit. Read each pair of words. Circle the word that is spelled correctly.

	A	B		A	B
1.	fale	fail	11.	same	saim
2.	ate	et	12.	gave	gaiv
3.	pepar	paper	13.	mal	mail
4.	wate	wait	14.	tren	train
5.	take	taik	15.	page	paig
6.	ren	rain	16.	age	aig
7.	meybe	maybe	17.	wake	waik
8.	face	fes	18.	late	lait
9.	afrade	afraid	19.	stait	state
10.	break	brek	20.	table	tayble

Read the four words in each row from Units 1–6. Underline the word that is spelled correctly.

	A	B	C	D
1.	fes	face	fais	fac
2.	trane	tran	train	tren
3.	brakefast	brakefest	breakfast	breakfest
4.	grade	gred	graid	gread
5.	again	agaen	agin	agein
6.	faimily	famely	famili	family
7.	paid	pade	baid	ped
8.	frech	freche	fresh	freshe
9.	peper	paper	paiper	peiper
10.	maike	mak	make	mek
11.	minit	menit	minite	minute
12.	afrad	afraid	afrade	afred
13.	exemple	exampl	exempl	example
14.	tgether	togthr	togather	togaither
15.	lait	laite	leate	late
16.	stait	stet	estaete	state
17.	doble	duble	double	doubl
18.	abble	ebble	aple	apple
19.	imbossible	impossible	imposibl	empossible
20.	moni	meney	money	mony

For more practice with the **writing** in this unit, go to NGL.Cengage.com/GWF.

Original Student Writing

Writing Your Ideas in Sentences or a Paragraph

Write five to ten sentences on your own paper. Write about people and their jobs. Use subject and object pronouns. For help, you can follow the examples in Activity 8 (page 102) and Activity 9 (page 103). (For more information about writing a paragraph, go to Appendix 4.)

Peer Editing

Exchange papers from the above activity. Read your partner's sentences. Then use Peer Editing Sheet 6 to make comments about the writing. Go to NGL.Cengage.com/GWF. There is a sample in Appendix 3.

For more practice with the **writing** in this unit, go to NGL.Cengage.com/GWF.

The Conjunction *and*

Two mountain bikers enjoy the mountains and weather in Chamonix, France.

OBJECTIVES **Grammar:** To learn about **and**
Vocabulary and Spelling: To study common words with the sound of <u>e</u> in <u>eat</u>
Writing: To write about your schedule for next week

Can you write about your activities for next week?

Grammar for Writing

The flag of Turkey is red **and** white.

The flag of Italy is green, white, **and** red.

And with Two Words

✓ You can use the conjunction **and** in English to connect two words or phrases. Study these examples.

Type of Words or Phrases	Examples	Examples with _and_
subjects	• **Lim** can play soccer. • **I** can play soccer.	**Lim and I** can play soccer.
objects	• Pinar speaks **Turkish**. • Pinar speaks **English**.	Pinar speaks **Turkish and English**.
verbs	• A teacher **plans** lessons. • A teacher **teaches** lessons.	A teacher **plans and teaches** lessons.
adjectives after **be**	• The flag of Canada is **red**. • The flag of Canada is **white**.	The flag of Canada is **red and white**.
adjectives before a noun	• We have **cold** weather in winter. • We have **wet** weather in winter.	We have **cold and wet** weather in winter.

ACTIVITY 1 Telling What _and_ Connects

In each sentence, put a box around the word **and.** Then circle the two words that **and** connects. On the lines, write N (noun), V (verb), A (adjective), or P (pronoun) to tell the type of words.

__V__ + __V__ **1.** My grandfather ⟨lives⟩ and ⟨works⟩ in London.

___ + ___ **2.** My cousins live in Texas and New Mexico.

___ + ___ **3.** My mother can cook simple and difficult kinds of Chinese dishes.

___ + ___ **4.** My mother and my father love each other very much.

___ + ___ **5.** My sister is smart and hard-working.

___ + ___ **6.** My sister is a smart and hard-working person.

___ + ___ **7.** My older brother likes to play checkers and hangman.

___ + ___ **8.** My younger brother and his friends play video games every day.

___ + ___ **9.** My aunt and I like to watch old movies.

___ + ___ **10.** Do you and your family do anything together on the weekends?

ACTIVITY 2 **Sentence Combining: Connecting Ideas with _and_**

Combine the two sentences with **and**. You may need to change some words and omit others.

1. I like apples. I like lemons.

    I like apples and lemons.

2. It is a yellow snake. It is a red snake.

3. I'm afraid of dogs. I'm afraid of spiders.

4. This sentence contains one verb. This sentence contains two nouns.

5. Lunch in Central America usually has rice. Lunch in Central America usually has beans.

6. She has classes in the morning. She has classes at night.

7. Make is a verb. Take is a verb.

8. Snake has five letters. Spain has five letters.

9. We eat eggs in the morning. We drink coffee in the morning.

10. January has 31 days. October has 31 days.

<u>And</u> with Three (or More) Words

✓ You can also use the conjunction **and** in English to connect three or more words or phrases.

✓ When there are three words, use a **comma** after the first word.

✓ Use a comma and **and** after the second word.

Examples	Examples with <u>and</u>
• The flag of Mexico is **green**. • The flag of Mexico is **white**. • The flag of Mexico is **red**.	The flag of Mexico is **green, white, and red**.
• **Thailand** is in Asia. • **Vietnam** is in Asia. • **Singapore** is in Asia.	**Thailand, Vietnam, and Singapore** are in Asia.

Common Student Mistakes

Sentence with Mistake X	The Problem	Correction ✓
<u>Miami, and Orlando</u> are in Florida.	comma with two words	**Miami and Orlando** are in Florida.
The salad has **lettuce tomatoes olives and** green onions.	commas missing with three or more words	The salad has lettuce, tomatoes, olives, and green onions.

ACTIVITY 3   Writing Sentences with More than One Subject

Combine the two sentences into one sentence. You can leave out some words, but make sure all the original ideas are in your sentence.

1. France is in Europe. England is in Europe.

    France and England are in Europe.
    _____

2. Basketball is a sport. Football is a sport.

    _____

3. An apple is a delicious kind of fruit. A banana is a delicious kind of fruit.

    _____

4. Go is a simple verb. Eat is a simple verb. Take is a simple verb.

    _____

5. The word **homework** has eight letters. The word **possible** has eight letters.

    _____

6. Yellow is a pretty color. Green is a pretty color. Blue is a pretty color.

_____

7. Isabella is a high school student. Sophia is a high school student.

_____

8. Istanbul is a city in Turkey. Ankara is a city in Turkey. Izmir is a city in Turkey.

_____

ACTIVITY 4 **Writing Sentences with More than One Object**

Combine the sentences to write one sentence. You can leave out some words, but make sure all the original ideas are in your sentence.

1. Lee speaks Chinese. Lee speaks Korean. Lee speaks English.

_____

2. I eat scrambled eggs for breakfast. I eat toast for breakfast. I eat fruit for breakfast.

_____

3. My children play football. My children play video games.

_____

4. Susan has a cat. Susan has five goldfish. Susan has a parrot.

_____

5. My brother can cook pasta well. My brother can cook steak well.

_____

6. Jose likes math. Jose likes science. Jose likes English. Jose likes history.

_____

ACTIVITY 5　Writing Sentences with More than One Adjective

Write a sentence about the colors of each flag. Be careful with capital letters, commas, and periods.

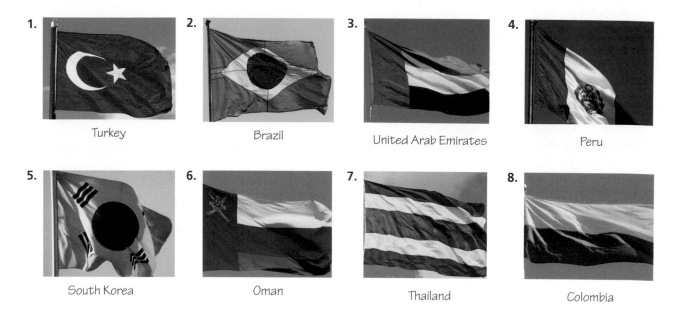

| 1. Turkey | 2. Brazil | 3. United Arab Emirates | 4. Peru |

| 5. South Korea | 6. Oman | 7. Thailand | 8. Colombia |

1. **The flag of Turkey is red and white.** _____

2. _____

3. _____

4. _____

5. _____

6. _____

7. _____

8. _____

ACTIVITY 6 Writing Sentences with More than One Verb

Combine the sentences to make one sentence. You can leave out some words, but make sure all the original ideas are in your sentence.

1. Franks lives in New York. Frank works in New York.

   Frank lives and works in New York.

2. Ducks swim. Ducks fly.

3. Maria buys the food. Maria cooks the food.

4. Maria buys the food on Sunday. Maria cooks the food on Monday.

5. Every morning I wake up before 7 a.m. Every morning I take a shower before 7 a.m. Every morning I get dressed before 7 a.m.

6. Students in this class read several books. Students in this class write two long reports. Students in this class take three big exams.

7. Alan makes a list of new English words. Alan studies it carefully.

8. Norah writes new English words in her notebook. Norah says them five times. Norah thinks of an example sentence for every word.

Write these sentences with correct capital letters, commas, and periods.

Some Information about Canada

1. the main cities in canada are toronto montreal and vancouver

_____

2. toronto vancouver and montreal have very busy airports

_____

3. the two official languages in canada are english and french

_____

4. many people live in ontario quebec british columbia and alberta

_____

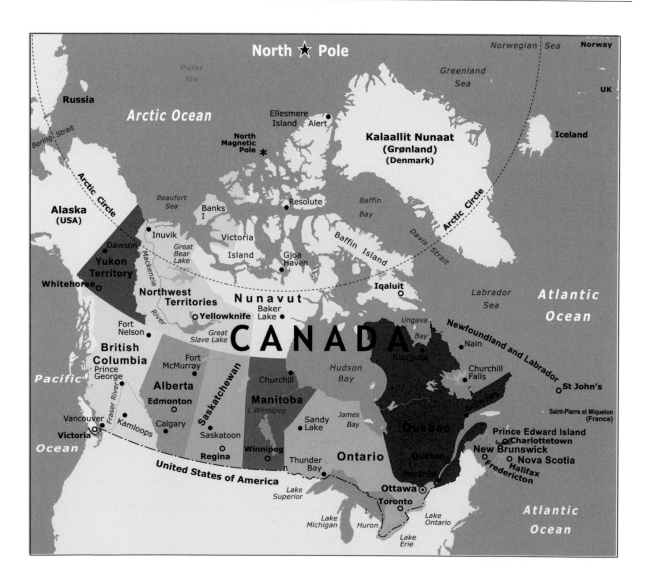

5. russia canada the united states china and brazil are very big countries

_____

6. the flag of canada is red and white

_____

7. four common names for girls in canada are emily emma olivia and sophia

_____

8. four common names for boys in canada are liam ethan jackson and jacob

_____

ACTIVITY 8 **Scrambled Sentences**

Change the order of the words to write a correct sentence. Be careful with spelling, capital letters, punctuation, and word order.

Flight 228 and Flight 226

1. goes new york from number to flight 228 paris

_____

2. every not this day flight is

_____

3. sunday friday flies and it thursday on monday

_____

4. seven new york flight between this paris takes and about hours

_____

5. dinner on eat a passengers this can snack breakfast and flight

_____

6. from goes 226 paris to flight new york

_____

7. for flight in three this london stops hours

_____

8. flies flight saturday 226 on and wednesday tuesday

_____

ACTIVITY 9 **Finding and Correcting 10 Mistakes**

Circle the ten mistakes. Then write the sentences correctly. The number in parentheses ( ) is the number of mistakes in that sentence. Be ready to explain your answers.

My Best Friends and Teammates

1. My best friends are Dave Jacob Daniel, and Joshua. (2)

   _____

2. Dave and I are in the sam class for English, history, and science. (1)

   _____

3. Dave and I have mathclass on monday and thursday. (3)

   _____

4. Jacob, Daniel, Joshua are no in our class. (2)

   _____

5. Dave and Jacob have fifteen year old. (2)

   _____

ACTIVITY 10 **Dictation**

You will hear six sentences three times. Listen carefully and write the six sentences. The number in parentheses ( ) is the number of words in the sentence. Be careful with capital letters and end punctuation.

1. _____ (7)

2. _____ (12)

3. _____ (8)

4. _____ (9)

5. _____ (11)

6. _____ (7)

ACTIVITY 11 **Practicing Grammar and Vocabulary in Model Writing**

Read the sentences in the paragraph very carefully. Fill in the missing words from the word bank. Circle the 18 letters that need to be capital letters. Add commas in the correct places. Then copy the paragraph on your own paper.

Sunday	Monday	Tuesday	Wednesday	Thursday	Friday	Saturday
1. ride bikes	1. math class	1. work 2. study	1. work 2. shop for food 3. study	1. math class	1. math class 2. ride bikes 3. call family	1. answer e-mails 2. read

to	next	and	many	and
on	once	want	us	schedule

A Busy Schedule for Next Week

1 my roommate _____ i do not have much free time next week.

2 _____ week will be really busy for _____. **3** This is our

_____ for next week. **4** we plan to do _____ different things.

5 we _____ to ride bikes on sunday and friday. **6** we have _____

work on tuesday and wednesday. **7** our math class is on monday thursday _____

friday. **8** we will read _____ saturday. **9** we shop for food only _____

a week.

ACTIVITY 12 **Guided Writing: Making Changes in a Model Writing**

Write the paragraph from Activity 11 again, but make the changes listed below and all other necessary changes.

Sentence 1. Change **I** to **his cousin.** You will need to make some changes with pronouns in other sentences, too.

Sentence 2. Change **really** to **very.** Change **us** to the correct pronoun.

Sentence 3. Change **This is** to **Here you can see.** Change **our** to the correct adjective.

Sentence 4. Change **we** to the correct pronoun here and in other sentences, too.

Sentence 5. Add **Monday** and **Saturday** in the correct places.

Sentence 6. Add **and study** in the correct place.

Sentence 7. Change **our** to the correct adjective. Add **really interesting** in the correct place.

Sentence 8. Add **answer e-mails and** in the correct place.

Sentence 9. Change **food** to **groceries.**

_____

_____

_____

_____

_____

_____

_____

_____

_____

_____

💻 For more practice with the **grammar** in this unit, go to NGL.Cengage.com/GWF.

Building Vocabulary and Spelling

Learning Words with the Sound of e in eat*

<u>e</u> = <u>ea</u>t   This sound is usually spelled with the letters **ea, ee, y, ey, ly, ese,** and others.

e a t

t e a

ACTIVITY 13 **Which Words Do You Know?**

This list has 62 words with the sound of <u>e</u> in <u>ea</u>t.

1. Notice the spelling patterns.

2. Check ✓ the words you know.

3. Look up new words in a dictionary. Write the meanings in your Vocabulary Notebook.

Common Words

GROUP 1:
Words spelled with **ea**

☐ 1. b e a c h

☐ 2. b e a n s

☐ 3. c h e a p

☐ 4. c l e a n

☐ 5. d r e a m

☐ 6. e a s y

☐ 7. e a t

☐ 8. h e a r

☐ 9. l e a v e

☐ 10. m e a n

☐ 11. m e a t

☐ 12. n e a r

☐ 13. p l e a s e

☐ 14. r e a d

☐ 15. s p e a k

☐ 16. t e a

*List is from: Spelling Vocabulary List © 2013 Keith Folse

- [ ] 17. teach
- [ ] 18. team
- [ ] 19. year

GROUP 2:
Words spelled with **ee**

- [ ] 20. between
- [ ] 21. cheese
- [ ] 22. coffee
- [ ] 23. feet
- [ ] 24. free
- [ ] 25. green
- [ ] 26. need
- [ ] 27. nineteen
- [ ] 28. sheep
- [ ] 29. sheet
- [ ] 30. sleep
- [ ] 31. sneeze
- [ ] 32. street
- [ ] 33. teeth
- [ ] 34. three
- [ ] 35. tree
- [ ] 36. week

GROUP 3:
Words spelled with **y**

- [ ] 37. baby
- [ ] 38. city
- [ ] 39. company
- [ ] 40. copy
- [ ] 41. country

- [ ] 42. early
- [ ] 43. every
- [ ] 44. family
- [ ] 45. necessary
- [ ] 46. ninety
- [ ] 47. story
- [ ] 48. university

GROUP 4:
Words spelled with **ey**

- [ ] 49. key
- [ ] 50. money

GROUP 5:
Words spelled with **ly**

- [ ] 51. finally
- [ ] 52. only
- [ ] 53. probably
- [ ] 54. really
- [ ] 55. slowly

GROUP 6:
Words spelled with **ese**

- [ ] 56. Chinese
- [ ] 57. Japanese

GROUP 7:
Other spellings

- [ ] 58. believe
- [ ] 59. email
- [ ] 60. people
- [ ] 61. pizza
- [ ] 62. receive

Use the list in Activity 13 to write the common word that matches the picture.

1. _____

2. _____

3. _____

4. _____

5. _____

6. _____

7. _____

8. _____

ACTIVITY 15 **Spelling Words with the Sound of e in eat**

Fill in the missing letters to spell words with the sound of **e** in **eat**. Then copy the correct word.

1. p___ple   ——————————

2. ninet__   ——————————

3. p__zza   ——————————

4. y___r   ——————————

5. l___ve   ——————————

6. countr__   ——————————

7. ninet___n   ——————————

8. mon___   ——————————

9. dr___m   ——————————

10. b___ns   ——————————

11. m___n   ——————————

12. t___ch   ——————————

ACTIVITY 16 **Writing Sentences with Vocabulary in Context**

Complete each sentence with the correct word from Activity 15. Then copy the sentence with correct capital letters and end punctuation.

1. miss jones and mr. mills .... at washington high school

———————————————————————————

2. my grandfather is ....years old

———————————————————————————

3. my brother is only .... years old

———————————————————————————

4. how many .... are in your family

———————————————————————————

5. i like .... with a lot of cheese and vegetables

———————————————————————————

6. there are 365 days in one ....

———————————————————————————

7. what time does the bus ....

———————————————————————————

8. people in brazil usually eat meat with rice and .... for lunch

———————————————————————————

9. the words **begin** and **start** .... the same thing

———————————————————————————

10. all students .... of a life without tests

_____

11. how much .... do you have with you today

_____

12. germany is a .... in europe

_____

ACTIVITY 17 **Scrambled Letters**

Change the order of the letters to write a word that has the sound of <u>e</u> in <u>ea</u>t.

_____ **1.** b b a y

_____ **2.** y t i c

_____ **3.** a r y s n s e c e

_____ **4.** c h e p a

_____ **5.** s i t y v e r u n i

_____ **6.** a e r y l

_____ **7.** n w t b e e e

_____ **8.** l o n y

_____ **9.** p a k e s

_____ **10.** c l a n e

_____ **11.** b e e l i v e

_____ **12.** r i c e e c v

_____ **13.** a c h e b

_____ **14.** w o s l l y

CD 1,
Track 14

ACTIVITY 18 **Spelling Practice**

Write the word that you hear. You will hear each word two times.

1. _____
2. _____
3. _____
4. _____
5. _____

6. _____
7. _____
8. _____
9. _____
10. _____

11. _____
12. _____
13. _____
14. _____
15. _____

ACTIVITY 19 Spelling Review: Which Word Is Correct?

This review covers the different ways of spelling the sound of **e** in **ea**t in this unit. Read each pair of words. Circle the word that is spelled correctly.

	A	B		A	B
1.	year	yeer	11.	fri	free
2.	drim	dream	12.	coffea	coffee
3.	sleap	sleep	13.	company	compani
4.	beans	beens	14.	easy	eesy
5.	finaly	finally	15.	early	earli
6.	eat	eet	16.	grean	green
7.	nineteen	ninteen	17.	nead	need
8.	leave	leeve	18.	teach	teech
9.	betwean	between	19.	Chainese	Chinese
10.	clean	cleen	20.	recive	receive

ACTIVITY 20 Cumulative Spelling Review

Read the four words in each row from Units 1–7. Underline the word that is spelled correctly.

	A	B	C	D
1.	clean	cleen	clene	clane
2.	tebl	tabl	table	teble
3.	nir	neer	nare	near
4.	gread	grade	gred	graid
5.	money	moni	monee	mney
6.	famili	famli	fammily	family
7.	peans	peens	beans	beens
8.	chep	chepe	cheap	chape
9.	esleep	eslip	sleap	sleep
10.	easy	easi	eazy	isi
11.	minit	minute	menit	minite
12.	afreid	afred	afraid	afread

A	B	C	D
13. ex<u>amble</u>	exemple	exambl	example
14. togeether	together	togather	togeathcr
15. cmpany	cmpani	company	compani
16. bottle	botle	bottel	bottil
17. esalat	salat	esalad	salad
18. trabel	travel	trubel	truvel
19. imposibl	empossible	imbossible	impossible
20. taksi	teksi	taxy	taxi

 For more practice with the **spelling and vocabulary** in this unit, go to NGL.Cengage.com/GWF.

Original Student Writing

Writing Your Ideas in Sentences or a Paragraph

Write five to ten sentences on your own paper. Write about your schedule for next week. Tell what you will do. Practice connecting words with **and.** For help, you can follow the examples in Activity 11 (page 123) and Activity 12 (page 124). (For more information about writing a paragraph, go to Appendix 4.)

Peer Editing

Exchange papers from the above activity. Read your partner's sentences.
Then use Peer Editing Sheet 7 to make comments about the writing. Go to NGL.Cengage.com/GWF.
There is a sample in Appendix 3.

 For more practice with the **writing** in this unit, go to NGL.Cengage.com/GWF.

Articles: *a, an, the, ---*

Student chefs prepare vegetables in woks in Hefei, Anhui Province, People's Republic of China.

OBJECTIVES Grammar: To learn about articles
Vocabulary and Spelling: To study common words with the sound of **i** in r**i**ce
Writing: To write about how to make a kind of food

Can you write about how to make a kind of food?

Grammar for Writing

London is **a** big city in **the** United Kingdom.
It is **an** interesting place for --- tourists to visit.

What Is an Article?

✓ The small words **a, an,** and **the** are called **articles**.

✓ Articles are used with nouns.

✓ Some nouns do not need an article. (---)

a / an	the
noun noun **A** <u>zebra</u> is **an** <u>animal</u>.	noun Lee and I are in **the** same <u>class</u>.
noun noun **A** <u>sentence</u> does not end with **a** <u>comma</u>.	noun noun What is **the** <u>title</u> of **the** <u>book</u>?

no article (---)
noun   noun I like --- <u>chicken</u> and --- <u>vegetables</u>.
noun   noun   noun   noun --- <u>Zebras</u> and --- <u>elephants</u> are --- <u>animals</u> in --- <u>Africa</u>.

Circle the 30 nouns in these sentences. Then underline the 16 articles. Write the number of articles in each sentence on the line by that sentence.

A Photo of a Park

_2_ **1.** This is a (photo) of a (park.)

_____ **2.** The park in this photo is near my house.

_____ **3.** There are not many people in the park.

_____ **4.** Today is Friday.

_____ **5.** You can see trees in the park.

_____ **6.** It is difficult to see the building behind this park.

_____ **7.** The green grass is very pretty.

_____ **8.** There is a man in the photo.

_____ **9.** He has a newspaper.

_____ **10.** The man likes to read in this park.

_____ **11.** He also likes to call his friends.

_____ **12.** The name of this park is Washington Park.

_____ **13.** There is a river in the park.

_____ **14.** We cannot see the river in this photo.

_____ **15.** Today is a great day at Washington Park.

Count and Non-Count (Mass) Nouns

In English there are two kinds of nouns: **count** and **non-count** (mass).

✓ You can count a **count noun**. For example, **year** is a **count noun** because you can say **one year, two years, three years**, etc.

✓ Count nouns have a singular form and a plural form. The most common way to write the plural of a count noun is with the letter **–s: books, words, days**. (Remember that some plurals are irregular: **men, women, children, feet, teeth, people.** See Unit 2, page 21.)

✓ You cannot count a **non-count noun**. For example, **money** is a **non-count noun** because you cannot say **one money, two moneys, three moneys**, etc.

✓ Non-count nouns do not have a singular or a plural form.

• You cannot use **a** or **an** before a non-count noun.

• You cannot add **–s** to a non-count noun.

Count Nouns	
Singular	**Plural**
a zebra	zebras
one zebra	two zebras
	some zebras
	many zebras
	how many zebras
	a lot of zebras
	a few zebras

Non-Count Nouns	
money	much money
some money	how much money
a lot of money	a little money

Here is a list of more common non-count nouns.

20 Non-Count Nouns You Need to Know		
1. advice	**8.** homework	**15.** peace
2. bread	**9.** information	**16.** rain
3. butter	**10.** luck	**17.** traffic
4. cash	**11.** mail	**18.** vocabulary
5. clothing	**12.** meat	**19.** weather
6. furniture	**13.** money	**20.** work
7. help	**14.** news	

ACTIVITY 2 **Recognizing Count and Non-Count Nouns**

Circle **count** or **non-count** to tell what the underlined noun is.

count   non-count   **1.** You have a <u>letter</u> on the table.

count   non-count   **2.** You have some <u>mail</u> on the table.

count   non-count   **3.** I have to do <u>homework</u>.

count   non-count   **4.** I have to take <u>a test</u>.

count   non-count   **5.** There are some <u>chickens</u> outside.

count   non-count   **6.** There is some <u>chicken</u> in the kitchen.

count   non-count   **7.** How much <u>money</u> do you have now?

count   non-count   **8.** How many <u>dollars</u> do you have now?

count non-count	**9.** They have a new <u>sofa</u>.	
count non-count	**10.** They have some new <u>furniture</u>.	
count non-count	**11.** This book has important <u>facts</u>.	
count non-count	**12.** This book has important <u>information</u>.	
count non-count	**13.** Please give me some <u>advice</u>.	
count non-count	**14.** Please give me your <u>opinion</u>.	
count non-count	**15.** There will be some bad <u>weather</u> tomorrow.	
count non-count	**16.** There will be a bad <u>storm</u> tomorrow.	

Articles with Singular and Plural Count Nouns

✓ Singular count nouns do not stand alone. You must use an article or another word before a singular count noun. For example, you can also use **this, that, these, those,** or a possessive adjective such as **my, you, his, her, our,** or **their.**

✓ Plural count nouns do not have **one, a,** or **an** before them.

Common Student Mistakes

Student Mistake X	Problem	Correct Example ✓
I **have new** car.	article missing	I have **a** new car.
My class has **a students** from many countries.	article with plural count noun	My class has **students** from many countries.

ACTIVITY 3 **Correcting Mistakes with Count Nouns**

The count nouns in these sentences have some mistakes. Correct the mistakes and write the sentences. Be careful with capitalization, articles, plurals, and end punctuation.

My Family

1. this is story about my family

_____

2. i have big family

_____

3. family has three brother and one sisters

_____

4. my first names is sara

_____

5. last name is mansour

_____

6. i am english student at kennedy college

_____

7. all my brother are high school student

_____

8. my sisters has good job

_____

9. she works at big company

_____

10. she is very important person there

_____

11. father and mother are very happy about a children

_____

A or An?

✓ The words **a** and **an** mean **one.**

✓ You use **a** or **an** with singular count nouns: **a** <u>dream</u>, **an** <u>action</u>

✓ You use **a** or **an** when the noun is not a specific person, place, or thing or when the noun is not the only person, place or thing: **a** <u>street</u>, **an** <u>apple</u>

✓ You use **an** before words that begin with a vowel sound, such as **a, i, e, o, u**: **an** <u>orange</u>

✓ You use **a** before words that begin with a consonant sound, such as **b, d, f, g, h**, etc: **a** <u>bridge</u>

Common Student Mistakes

Student Mistake **X**	Problem	Correct Example ✓
Lima is **the** city in Peru.	wrong article for general meaning	Lima is **a** city in Peru.
A elephant is a big animal.	wrong article before word that begins with a vowel sound	**An** elephant is a big animal.
I teach at **an university** in London.	wrong article before word that does not begin with a vowel sound	I teach at **a** university in London. (**University** does not begin with a vowel sound.)

ACTIVITY 4 Using Correct Articles in Noun Phrases

Write **a, an,** or --- on the line to show what comes before the words.

1. _____ book
2. _____ green book
3. _____ English book
4. _____ books
5. _____ green books
6. ___ English books

7. _____ animal
8. _____ animals
9. _____ big animal
10. _____ big animals
11. _____ cash
12. _____ money

13. _____ coin
14. _____ examples
15. _____ easy examples
16. _____ test
17. _____ exam
18. _____ hard exam

ACTIVITY 5 Writing Simple Definition Sentences

Draw a line from a noun in column 1 to the definition it goes with in column 2. Then write a sentence that explains what the first noun is. Be careful with articles, verbs, capitalization, and final punctuation.

1	2
1. apple	animal in Africa
2. e-mail	colorful bird
3. onion	vegetable
4. dictionary	electronic message
5. zebra	delicious fruit
6. nickel	pretty flower
7. rose	useful book
8. bee	coin
9. parrot	insect with wings
10. park	great place

1. An apple is a delicious fruit. _____
2. _____
3. _____
4. _____
5. _____
6. _____

7. _____

8. _____

9. _____

10. _____

The

✓ You can use **the** with all three kinds of nouns:
  - singular count noun: **the** <u>cup</u>
  - plural count noun: **the** <u>cups</u>
  - non-count noun: **the** <u>money</u>

✓ Use **the** when you write about a specific person, place, or thing.

Sentences with <u>the</u>	Explanations
I have a pen and a pencil. **The** pen is red.	We use **the** when we write about something for the second time.
Reiko, please put **the** tea pot on **the** stove.	We use **the** when the speaker and the listener are talking about the same thing.
I live in a great apartment. **The** kitchen is very big.	We use **the** when the noun is a part of something else.

✓ Do not use **the** when you write about a general person, place, or thing.

Sentences without <u>the</u>	Explanations
I like **roses**. I like **the roses** in your garden.	**Roses** in the first sentences means all roses in general. **The roses** in the second sentence is specific.
My favorite color is **blue**. **The blue** in the French flag is different from **the blue** in the American flag.	**Blue** in the first sentences means blue in general. **The blue** in the second sentence is specific.

ACTIVITY 6 Using the in Context

Fill in the missing words from the word bank. You will not use every word. You may use some words more than once.

English	second	first	visitors	people	reasons
the English	the second	the first	the visitors	the people	two reasons

Why I Want to Learn English

1. I want to learn _____ for _____.

2. _____ reason is my family.

3. My children can already speak _____ very well.

4. I want to understand them better.

5. _____ reason is my job.

6. In my job, I work with _____ every day.

7. Most of them speak only _____.

8. I need to speak good _____ with these visitors.

9. Also, most of _____ in my office speak more than one language well.

10. I will work very hard to improve my _____.

ACTIVITY 7 Using Articles in Context

Read this short recipe to make something delicious. Fill in the blanks with **a, an, the,** or ---.

How I Make My Favorite Sandwich

1. I like _____ sandwiches.

2. I usually eat _____ sandwich for _____ lunch.

3. Many people eat _____ sandwiches for _____ lunch.

4. I sometimes eat _____ sandwich for _____ breakfast.

5. My favorite sandwich is _____ tomato sandwich with _____ mustard.

6. It is easy to make _____ tomato sandwich.

7. You need _____ tomato, _____ bread, and _____ mustard.

8. I put a little mustard on _____ bread.

9. I cut _____ tomato into _____ slices.

10. I put two or three of _____ tomato slices on _____ bread.

11. Now _____ sandwich is ready to eat.

12. You also need _____ delicious drink to go with _____ great sandwich.

The with Places

✓ You use **the** with the names of some places.
--- New York is in **the United States.**

The Nile River is in --- Egypt.

✓ You use **the** with certain geography words, including all mountains, deserts, and bodies of water (except lakes).

✓ Most country names do not use **the.** You do use **the** with places that sound plural (usually ending in **–s** or containing words such as **united, kingdom, republic**).

the United States	the Kingdom of Saudi Arabia
the Philippines	the Republic of South Korea
the Netherlands	the United Arab Emirates

When to Write the

the		---	
rivers	the Amazon River	lakes	--- Lake Victoria
oceans	the Pacific Ocean	countries	--- South Korea
areas (of a place)	the coast	continents	--- South America
deserts	the Sahara Desert	states	--- California
groups of mountains	the Andes Mountains	one mountain	--- Mount Everest
schools with **of**	the University of Texas	schools	--- Iowa State University
hotels	the Highland Hotel	cities	--- New York
museums	the Louvre		

ACTIVITY 8   Using <u>the</u> for Places

Write **the** or --- on the lines. Then circle **True** or **False** for each fact. (Hint: Only six sentences have true information.)

A Geography Test

True   False   **1.** _____ Washington, D.C., is the capital of _____ United Kingdom.

True   False   **2.** _____ Dubai is in _____ United Arab Emirates.

True   False   **3.** _____ Mediterranean Sea is between _____ Africa and _____ Europe.

True   False   **4.** _____ Nile River is in _____ Morocco.

True   False   **5.** _____ Hanoi and _____ Ho Chi Minh City are in _____ Philippines.

True   False   **6.** _____ Buenos Aires is the capital of _____ Argentina.

True   False   **7.** _____ Busan and _____ Seoul are in _____ South Korea.

True   False   **8.** _____ Andes Mountains are in _____ North America.

True   False   **9.** _____ Berlin is the capital of _____ Turkey.

True   False   **10.** _____ British Columbia is in _____ Canada.

True   False   **11.** _____ Oman is a country in _____ Middle East.

True   False   **12.** _____ Atacama Desert is in _____ Colombia and _____ Brazil.

ACTIVITY 9   Writing Sentences with <u>the</u> for Places

Six sentences from Activity 8 are false. Write the correct information for those six sentences here. Be careful with capitalization, articles, and periods.

1. _____

2. _____

3. _____

4. _____

5. _____

6. _____

Common Student Mistakes

Student Mistake X	Problem	Correct Example ✓
My favorite sport is **the** football.	article with general words	My favorite sport **is football**.
Please **put apples** here.	article missing with a specific noun	Please put **the** apples here.
I want to study English **in United States**.	article missing with some places	I want to study English in **the** United States.

ACTIVITY 10 **Correcting Sentences with Articles**

Write these sentences with correct capital letters, articles, commas, and periods.

My Friend Maria

1. my best friend is maria garcia

_____

2. maria is history teacher in her country

_____

3. she also wants to teach spanish one day

_____

4. now she is student again

_____

5. she and i study spanish in same class

_____

6. maria is from philippines

_____

7. philippines is country in asia

_____

8. it is in pacific ocean

_____

9. it is near malaysia indonesia and vietnam

_____

10. maria is great student

_____

11. she is best student in our spanish class

_____

12. she will be great spanish teacher in her school in philippines

_____

ACTIVITY 11 **Scrambled Sentences**

Change the order of the words to write a correct sentence. Be careful with spelling, capital letters, punctuation, and word order.

Cooking Scrambled Eggs

1. today i make want to eggs scrambled

_____

2. i eggs and a little need two milk

_____

3. oil some pepper i also need some some salt and

_____

4. mix the eggs and the i milk bowl together in a

_____

5. i add salt pepper and the the

_____

6. everything together one more i mix time

_____

7. a i oil in put the pan

_____

8. put i the the pan liquid in

_____

9. i for a few cook minutes the eggs

_____

10. my eat now i can breakfast delicious

_____

ACTIVITY 12 Finding and Correcting 10 Mistakes

Circle the ten mistakes. Then write the sentences correctly. The number in parentheses ( ) is the number of mistakes in that sentence. Be ready to explain your answers.

Our Three Books

1. We have three book for our English class. (1)

   _____

2. We have writing book a reading book, and a grammar book. (2)

   _____

3. the reading book is many words difficult. (3)

   _____

4. The writing book, and the grammar book are no very easy. (2)

   _____

5. The reading book has an interesting stories from the Turkey, Japan, and Brazil. (2)

   _____

CD 2, Track 1 **ACTIVITY 13** **Dictation**

You will hear six sentences three times. Listen carefully and write the six sentences. The number in parentheses ( ) is the number of words in the sentence. Be careful with capital letters, commas, and end punctuation.

1. _____ (9)

2. _____ (6)

3. _____ (7)

4. _____ (8)

5. _____ (8)

6. _____ (7)

ACTIVITY 14 **Practicing Grammar and Vocabulary in Model Writing**

Read the sentences in the paragraph very carefully. Fill in the missing words from the word bank. Circle the ten letters that need to be capital letters. Then copy the paragraph on your own paper.

mix	the egg	the salt	tuna salad	make
egg	the tuna	add	the tuna salad	tuna

Making Tuna Salad

1 my favorite thing to eat is _____ . **2** it is easy to _____ tuna salad.

3 you need a can of _____ 4 spoons of mayonnaise 1 spoon of mustard a little

salt and a little pepper. **4** you can also use 2 spoons of chopped onions and a chopped hard-boiled

_____ . **5** put _____ in a bowl. **6** then _____ the

mayonnaise and the mustard to the tuna. **7** now add the onions and _____ .

8 now add _____ and the pepper. **9** next, _____ all of these together.

10 _____ is now ready for your guests to eat.

Write the paragraph from Activity 14 again, but make the changes listed below and all other necessary changes.

<u>Sentence 1</u>. Change **tuna** to **chicken**, and then make changes in the other sentences.

<u>Sentence 2</u>. Change **easy** to **not very difficult**.

<u>Sentence 3</u>. Change **1** to **2.**

<u>Sentence 4</u>. Add **green** to the word **onions**.

<u>Sentence 5</u>. Add the adjective **large** in the correct place.

<u>Sentences 7 and 8</u>. Combine these two sentences into one sentence.

<u>Sentence 9</u>. Change **all of these** to **everything**.

<u>Sentence 10</u>. Change **guests** to **friends and neighbors**.

_____

_____

_____

_____

_____

_____

_____

_____

_____

For more practice with the **grammar** in this unit, go to NGL.Cengage.com/GWF.

Building Vocabulary and Spelling

Learning Words with the Sound of $\boxed{i}$ in $\boxed{rice}$ *

i = r **i** c **e**   This sound is usually spelled with the letters **i** + consonant + final **e, y, ight, ind, ie,** and others.

r i c e

c r y

l i g h t

ACTIVITY 16 Which Words Do You Know?

This list has 52 common words with the sound of **i** in r**i**ce.

1. Notice the spelling patterns.

2. Check (✓) the words you know.

3. Look up new words in a dictionary. Write the meanings in your Vocabulary Notebook.

Common Words

GROUP 1:
Words spelled with **i** + consonant + final e

☐ 1. a r r i v e
☐ 2. b i k e
☐ 3. d e c i d e
☐ 4. d r i v e
☐ 5. f i r e
☐ 6. i c e
☐ 7. i n s i d e
☐ 8. k n i f e

☐ 9. l i f e
☐ 10. l i k e
☐ 11. m i n e
☐ 12. n i c e
☐ 13. n i n e
☐ 14. p r i c e
☐ 15. r i c e
☐ 16. r i d e

☐ 17. s i z e
☐ 18. s m i l e
☐ 19. t i m e
☐ 20. t i m e s
☐ 21. w h i t e
☐ 22. w i f e
☐ 23. w r i t e

*List is from: Spelling Vocabulary List © 2013 Keith Folse

GROUP 2:
Words that end with **y**

- [ ] 24. b y
- [ ] 25. c r y
- [ ] 26. d r y
- [ ] 27. f l y
- [ ] 28. J u l y
- [ ] 29. m y
- [ ] 30. s k y
- [ ] 31. t r y
- [ ] 32. w h y

GROUP 3:
Words that end in **ight**

- [ ] 33. f i g h t
- [ ] 34. f l i g h t
- [ ] 35. l i g h t
- [ ] 36. n i g h t
- [ ] 37. r i g h t
- [ ] 38. t o n i g h t

GROUP 4:
Words that end in **ind**

- [ ] 39. b e h i n d
- [ ] 40. f i n d
- [ ] 41. k i n d

GROUP 5:
Words that end in **ie**

- [ ] 42. d i e
- [ ] 43. l i e
- [ ] 44. t i e

GROUP 6:
Other spellings

- [ ] 45. b u y
- [ ] 46. e y e
- [ ] 47. h i g h
- [ ] 48. I
- [ ] 49. i d e a
- [ ] 50. q u i e t
- [ ] 51. p i l o t
- [ ] 52. s i l e n t

ACTIVITY 17 **Matching Words and Pictures**

Use the list in Activity 16 to write the common word that matches the picture.

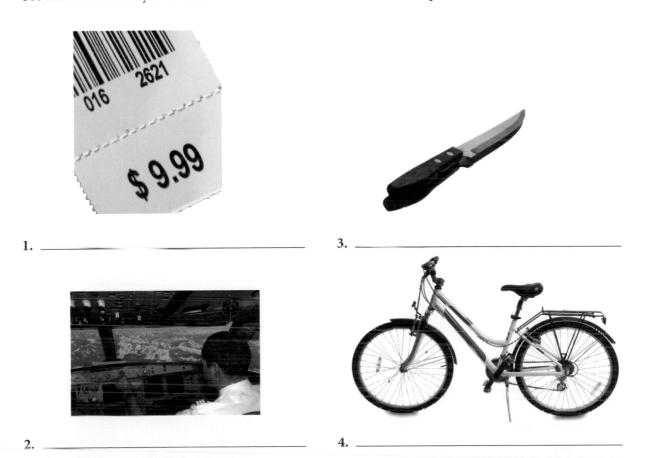

1. _____

2. _____

3. _____

4. _____

5. _____   **7.** _____

6. _____   **8.** _____

ACTIVITY 18 **Spelling Words with the Sound of i̱ in rīce̱**

Fill in the missing letters to spell words with the sound of **i̱** in r**īce̱**. Then copy the correct word.

1. l __ k __   _____   **7.** r __ d __   _____

2. h __   _____   **8.** __ dea   _____

3. fl __ t   _____   **9.** b __ y   _____

4. dr __   _____   **10.** b __   _____

5. t __ m __   _____   **11.** dr __ v __   _____

6. f __ nd   _____   **12.** wh __   _____

Complete each sentence with the correct word from Activity 18. Then copy the sentence with correct capital letters and punctuation.

1. i can't ………… my keys

   _____

2. what ………… does the ………… for london leave

   _____

3. ………… did you try to quit your old job

   _____

4. many of my cousins and i stay in touch ………… e-mail

   _____

5. we would ………… to ………… a new car this year

   _____

6. we have an ………… about how to fix the problem

   _____

7. it is not very difficult to ………… a small car

   _____

8. the opposite of wet is …………

   _____

9. do you ………… your bike to school every day

   _____

10. the price of a brand new car is …………

    _____

ACTIVITY 20 **Scrambled Letters**

Change the order of the letters to write a word that has the sound of **i** in n**i**ce.

_____ 1. s t m e i	_____ 8. k n i d
_____ 2. m e i n	_____ 9. e i u q t
_____ 3. t h i w e	_____ 10. h h i g
_____ 4. r g h t i	_____ 11. h n d b e i
_____ 5. l u J y	_____ 12. z s e i
_____ 6. e n t l i s	_____ 13. e l d
_____ 7. s d e n i i	_____ 14. l i m s e

CD 2,
Track 2 **ACTIVITY 21** **Spelling Practice**

Write the word that you hear. You will hear each word two times.

1. _____   6. _____   11. _____

2. _____   7. _____   12. _____

3. _____   8. _____   13. _____

4. _____   9. _____   14. _____

5. _____   10. _____   15. _____

ACTIVITY 22 **Spelling Review: Which Word Is Correct?**

This review covers the different ways of spelling **i** in n**i**ce in this unit. Read each pair of words. Circle the word that is spelled correctly.

	A	B		A	B
1.	bui	buy	11.	nait	night
2.	die	di	12.	like	lik
3.	behynd	behind	13.	hiegh	high
4.	lait	light	14.	tims	times
5.	wy	why	15.	ais	ice
6.	July	Juli	16.	right	rigt
7.	arriv	arrive	17.	quiet	queit
8.	rais	rice	18.	wite	white
9.	ey	eye	19.	knife	knighfe
10.	siz	size	20.	slent	silent

ACTIVITY 23 **Cumulative Spelling Review**

Read the four words in each row from Units 1–8. Underline the word that is spelled correctly.

	A	B	C	D
1.	wi	why	whi	wy
2.	inside	insde	insaid	insighd
3.	moni	muney	mney	money
4.	usuali	usally	usully	usually

	A	B	C	D
5.	behnd	bihind	behind	bhind
6.	nife	naif	knif	knife
7.	grade	gred	graid	gread
8.	smail	esmile	esmail	smile
9.	saied	sed	sayed	said
10.	Juli	July	Julai	Jly
11.	breakfast	breakfest	brekfast	brekfest
12.	evrithing	everythng	everything	evrithng
13.	tonight	tonit	tonite	tnight
14.	idea	idee	aidea	eyedee
15.	again	agan	egain	agean
16.	theye	theiy	they	thay
17.	deside	desid	decide	decid
18.	studi	study	estudi	estudy
19.	soks	socks	saks	sawks
20.	dribe	drive	driv	drib

💻 For more practice with the **spelling and vocabulary** in this unit, go to NGL.Cengage.com/GWF.

Original Student Writing

Writing Your Ideas in Sentences or a Paragraph

Write five to ten sentences on your own paper. Write about how to make some kind of food. It can be a simple dish or anything you want. Use articles correctly. For help, you can follow the examples in Activity 14 (page 148) and Activity 15 (page 149). (For more information about writing a paragraph, go to Appendix 4.)

Peer Editing

Exchange papers from the above activity. Read your partner's sentences.
Then use Peer Editing Sheet 8 to make comments about the writing. Go to NGL.Cengage.com/GWF.
There is a sample in Appendix 3.

💻 For more practice with the **writing** in this unit, go to NGL.Cengage.com/GWF.

Prepositions

A gargoyle looks down over the city and the Seine River in Paris, France.

OBJECTIVES Grammar: To learn about prepositions
Vocabulary and Spelling: To study common words with the sound of **o** in **hell_o_**
Writing: To write about things to see and do in your city

Can you write about things to see and do In your city?

Grammar for Writing

The man is **on** a mountain **in** Switzerland.

What Is a Preposition?

✓ **A preposition** is a word that shows the relationship between a noun and other words in the sentence.

✓ Common prepositions include:

after   from   of   to   before   in   on   with

✓ A **prepositional phrase** is a preposition and its noun (or pronoun) object.

prep + object	prep + object	prep + object
after my <u>class</u>	**in** <u>Japan</u>	**with** my <u>best friend</u>

✓ Prepositions often answer **where, when,** or **how.**

where?	We live **in Tokyo.** Our apartment is **near a big park.**
when?	I was born **in 1992.** I was born **on May 2nd.**
how?	He likes to write **with a blue pen.** He likes to work **by himself.**

20 Prepositions You Need to Know*

1. of	What is the name **of** your book?	
2. to	I go **to** the park once a week.	
3. in	**PLACE**: We live **in** China. **TIME**: I was born **in** September.	
4. for	This clock is a gift **for** you.	
5. with	I go to the store **with** my mother.	
6. on	**PLACE**: The pencils are **on** the table. **TIME**: I work **on** Monday.	
7. at	**PLACE**: My sister works **at** Union Bank. **TIME**: She starts her job **at** 9 a.m.	
8. by	We live **by** the river.	
9. from	I am **from** San Francisco.	
10. up	This bus goes **up** that mountain.	
11. about	This story is **about** two people.	
12. than	Gold is more expensive **than** silver.	
13. after	We study **after** school.	
14. before	I usually go to sleep **before** midnight.	
15. down	She is walking **down** the steps.	
16. between	The United States is **between** Canada and Mexico.	
17. under	My shoes are **under** the sofa.	
18. since	I have worked here **since** 2010.	
19. without	My father likes coffee **without** sugar.	
20. near	I live **near** the beach.	

Based on the General Service List, Corpus of Contemporary American English, and other corpus sources.

Underline the 26 prepositional phrases in these sentences. Circle the prepositions.

My Student Life

1. I am a high school student (in) Singapore.

2. I go to Mayflower Secondary School.

3. I am in my last year at this school.

4. I begin my trip from home to school at 7 a.m.

5. My friends and I go to school by bus.

6. Our first class begins at 8 a.m.

7. My last class ends at 3 p.m.

8. After school, I take a bus to my house.

9. On the trip between my school and my house, I listen to music.

10. I eat dinner with my family at 7 p.m.

11. Before dinner, I usually study.

12. On Monday and Friday, I study from 4 p.m. to 7 p.m.

13. On some days, I study after dinner, too.

14. I study more on Monday than any other day.

at, on, in: Three Common Prepositions of Time

✓ Common prepositions of time are **at, on,** and **in**.

✓ You use **at** for clock time.

✓ You use **on** for days and dates.

✓ You use **in** for months, years, seasons, and longer periods of time.

AT
at 10 o'clock
at midnight

ON
on Monday
on May 30th
on my birthday

IN
in May
in 2015
in this decade

ACTIVITY 2   Prepositional Phrases of Time with <u>at</u>, <u>on</u>, <u>in</u>

In A, write **at, on,** or **in** to complete the prepositional phrase of time. In B, write an original sentence with each prepositional phrase.

A.

1. _____ Monday
2. _____ 9 o'clock
3. _____ midnight
4. _____ 2012
5. _____ Friday
6. _____ January 1st
7. _____ January
8. _____ summer

B.

1. _____

2. _____

3. _____

4. _____

5. _____

6. _____

7. _____

8. _____

ACTIVITY 3   <u>at</u>, <u>on</u>, <u>in</u>: Scrambled Sentences with Prepositional Phrases of Time

Change the order of the words to write a correct sentence. Be careful with capital letters and punctuation.

1. at french o'clock 10 my begins class

   _____

2. at boston leaves the bus for nine

   _____

3. july family a my trip in takes

   _____

4. sunday show is on favorite our TV

   _____

5. maria and norah i 1985 born were in

   _____

6. birthday is in my january

_____

7. i go at sleep to midnight

_____

8. tuesday and have class english on monday wednesday we

_____

<u>at</u>, <u>on</u>, <u>in</u>: Three Common Prepositions of Place

✓ Common prepositions of place are **at, on,** and **in**.

✓ You use **at** for specific places, including addresses.

✓ You use **on** for streets.

✓ You use **in** for an area, a state, a country, a continent.

AT — **at** Union Bank / **at** 335 Main Street

ON — **on** Main Street

IN — **in** Orlando / **in** Florida / **in** the United States

ACTIVITY 4 **Prepositional Phrases of Place with <u>at</u>, <u>on</u>, <u>in</u>**

In A, write **at, on,** or **in** to complete the prepositional phrase of place. In B, write an original sentence with each prepositional phrase.

A.

1. _____ Union Bank

2. _____ Pine Street

3. _____ 277 Pine Street

4. _____ Los Angeles

5. _____ California

6. _____ the United States

7. _____ Minnesota University

8. _____ Shoes for Less

B.

1. _____

2. _____

3. _____

4. _____

5. _____

6. _____

7. _____

8. _____

ACTIVITY 5 **Writing Two Related Sentences**

Use the city and country in each item to write two sentences.

Step 1. In the first sentence, add the words **we live** to tell where you and your family live.

Step 2. In the second sentence, tell the location of the city. Use the words **is a city** in your sentence.

Be careful with capitalization, punctuation, articles, and prepositions.

1. athens – greece _We live in Athens.   Athens is a city in Greece._ _____

   _____

2. osaka – japan _____

   _____

3. rabat – morocco _____

   _____

4. lima – peru _____

   _____

5. seattle – united states _____

   _____

6. dubai – united arab emirates _____

   _____

7. chihuahua – mexico _____

   _____

8. amsterdam – netherlands

   _____

ACTIVITY 6 **Writing about the Location of Places on a Map**

Write **at** or **on** to complete the prepositional phrase of place. Then write a sentence with the prepositional phrase to tell the location of the business on the map.

A Business Map of Downtown

1. ___at___ 105 Maple Street   (Tim's Bookstore)

   Tim's Bookstore is at 105 Maple Street.

2. _____ Maple Street   (Pretty Flowers)

3. _____ Pine Street   (two restaurants)

4. _____ 101 Pine Street   (Gold Things)

5. _____ 101 Maple Street   (First City Bank)

6. _____ 107 Pine Street   (Shoes for Less)

_____

7. _____ Maple Street   (my bank and the post office)

_____

8. _____ Pine Street   (Gold Things, Fun Toys, Shoes for Less)

_____

Word Order: Place and Time in the Same Sentence

✓ When an English sentence has both a prepositional phrase of place and a prepositional phrase of time, you <u>usually</u> put **place before time**. (An easy way to remember this is **P comes before T** in the alphabet: **Place before Time.**)

Examples of Place before Time .	
I go **to my office**. (place) I go **at 7 a.m.** (time)	place time I go **to my office** **at 7 a.m**.
He studies **at 8 o'clock**. (place) He studies **in the library**. (time)	place time He studies **in the library** **at 8 o'clock**.

ACTIVITY 7 **Scrambled Sentences with Prepositional Phrases of Place and Time**

Change the order of the words to write a correct sentence. Be careful with capital letters and punctuation.

1. we to went in london 1999

_____

2. supermarket saturday vegetables at mother on my buys the morning

_____

3. the the melissa library in at afternoon i and study

_____

4. one students lunch in from eat noon to the cafeteria o'clock

_____

5. want to i new study english in york in 2020

_____

6. in we to move apartment november will another

_____

Word Order: Beginning a Sentence with a Prepositional Phrase

✓ A sentence can begin with a prepositional phrase.

✓ You use a comma after a prepositional phrase that begins a sentence.

✓ You do not use a comma for prepositional phrases at the end of a sentence.

At the Beginning of the Sentence	At the End of the Sentence
In Japan, people drive on the left side of the road.	People drive on the left side of the road **in Japan.**
In April, Japanese students start school.	Japanese students start school **in April.**

✓ When writers begin a sentence with a prepositional phrase, they want to emphasize that information. The basic meaning is the same as when the prepositional phrase is near the end of the sentence.

ACTIVITY 8   Writing Sentences that Start with Prepositional Phrases

Write each sentence again. Move the last prepositional phrase to the beginning of your new sentence. Be careful with capitalization, word order, and punctuation.

1. My sister has English class on Monday.

     _____

2. Lynn, Jane, and Karen usually take bus 28 on Tuesday and Thursday.

     _____

3. You can see a better map of Asia on page 237.

     _____

4. Adjectives come before nouns in English.

     _____

5. Kevin and I have a very important meeting at 7 o'clock tonight.

     _____

6. U.S. citizens have to get a tourist visa for Russia, China, and Brazil.

     _____

Common Preposition Combinations after Verbs, Adjectives, and Nouns

✓ Sometimes a verb, an adjective, or a noun requires a certain preposition after it. You must memorize these word combinations.

Verbs	**1.** listen to	At night, I **listen to** music.
	2. look at	My brother likes to **look at** maps.
	3. look for	We will **look for** a new apartment.
	4. wait for	I **wait for** the bus here.
Adjectives	**1.** afraid of	They are **afraid of** snakes.
	2. different from	Chinese is **different from** Japanese.
	3. famous for	Paris is **famous for** the Eiffel Tower.
	4. far from	Alaska is **far from** Brazil.
	5. full of	This shopping center is **full of** teenagers on the weekend.
	6. happy about	We are very **happy about** your new job.
	7. important for	Eating good food is **important for** everyone.
	8. interested in	Are you **interested in** sports?
	9. married to	Lukas is **married to** Leila.
	10. necessary for	Water and light are **necessary for** plants to grow.
	11. ready for	We are **ready for** our trip to Spain.
	12. similar to	French is **similar to** Italian.
	13. sorry about	I am very **sorry about** your problems.
	14. tired of	The students are **tired of** tests every week.
	15. worried about	Mr. Miller is **worried about** his money problems.
Nouns	**1.** the cause of	No one knows **the cause of** the fire.
	2. the center of	The capital of the United States is not in **the center of** the country.
	3. the cost of	**The cost of** everything goes up every year.
	4. the difference between	Do you know **the difference between** a noun and a pronoun?
	5. an example of	*Kick* is **an example of** a word that begins and ends with the same letter.
	6. the matter with	What is **the matter with** you?
	7. the middle of	The horse is in **the middle of** the street.
	8. the price of	**The price of** food in that country is very expensive.
	9. a problem with	There is **a problem with** my phone.
	10. a question about	I have **a question about** my electricity bill.
	11. the same as	Your grade is **the same as** my grade.

Practicing Prepositions after Verbs, Adjectives, and Nouns

Underline the correct preposition in each sentence.

1. John is married (at, for, to, with) Beth.

2. Bolivia is an example (as, of, for, in) a country without a coast.

3. At my university, students spend a lot of time looking (at, for, in, of) a parking space.

4. We will wait (by, for, out, to) you right here. Please come back quickly.

5. I am ready (in, from, for, on) my big test tomorrow.

6. Pink is similar (at, for, in, to) red.

7. Green is different (at, for, from, to) red.

8. I do not want to have a problem (of, for, in, with) my visa.

9. I like to listen (for, in, on, to) music in my car.

10. We like sports. We are very interested (of, in, on, with) European and South American soccer.

Common Student Mistakes

Student Mistake X	Problem	Correct Example ✓
Miami and Orlando are **on** Florida.	wrong preposition	Miami and Orlando are **in** Florida.
I like to **listen music** in my car.	preposition missing	I like to listen **to** music in my car.
Ed goes **on Tuesdays and Thursdays to his classes**.	time before place	Ed goes **to his classes on Tuesdays and Thursdays.**
With my friend I went to the beach last weekend.	comma missing after prepositional phrase that begins a sentence	With my friend, I went to the beach last weekend.

Scrambled Sentences

Change the order of the words to write a correct sentence. Be careful with spelling, capital letters, punctuation, and word order.

Comparing Three Long Flights from New York

1. schedules are long for three the flights these

_____

2. these on three all international airlines of are flights

_____

3. from number new york goes 434 to flight london

_____

4. and 8 a.m. leaves it at it 8 p.m. arrives

_____

5. goes york 221 flight tokyo to number new from

_____

6. arrives the 3:30 p.m. at leaves this next 11:30 a.m. at flight day one and

_____

7. lima 395 goes new from flight to york

_____

8. at arrives it 8 p.m. and 9 a.m. at leaves

_____

9. stops hours in this panama two flight for

_____

ACTIVITY 11 **Finding and Correcting 10 Mistakes**

Circle the ten mistakes. Then write the sentences correctly. The number in parentheses ( ) is the number of mistakes in that sentence. Be ready to explain your answers.

Things I Want To Do

1. I am student at Washington High School. (1)

_____

2. My class favorite is the geography. (2)

_____

3. In the future I want to visit the pyramids near from Cairo in Egypt. (2)

_____

4. I want to walk up a mountain at Chile. (1)

_____

5. I want to see the buildings famous at Paris. (2)

_____

6. After Paris I want to go Japan to ride on the fast trains there. (2)

_____

CD 2,
Track 3 **ACTIVITY 12** **Dictation**

You will hear six sentences three times. Listen carefully and write the six sentences. The number in parentheses ( ) is the number of words. Be careful with capital letters and end punctuation.

1. _____ (7)

2. _____ (7)

3. _____ (8)

4. _____ (9)

5. _____ (11)

6. _____ (10)

ACTIVITY 13 Practicing Grammar and Vocabulary in Model Writing

Read the sentences in the paragraph very carefully. Fill in the missing words from the word bank. Circle the 24 letters that need to be capital letters. Then copy the paragraph on your own paper.

than	of	on	in	from	at
in	and	in	with	for	also

Tourists in Paris

1 marie lives _____ an apartment in paris. **2** her apartment is

_____ the tenth floor of a very big apartment building. **3** _____ her

apartment, she can see paris well. **4** _____ example, her apartment is near the eiffel

tower. **5** every year more _____ fifteen million tourists come to paris.

6 most tourists visit _____ the summer. **7** it is difficult to find a good hotel room

_____ july. **8** they come _____ a long list of things to do in paris.

9 many people like to take a picture _____ the eiffel tower. **10** they _____

like to visit the many old buildings in the city. **11** some tourists look _____ the famous

paintings in the louvre museum. **12** tourists love paris, _____ marie loves her city, too.

ACTIVITY 14 Guided Writing: Making Changes in Model Writing

Write the paragraph from Activity 13 again, but make the changes listed below and all other necessary changes.

<u>Sentence 1</u>. Change **Paris** to a new city that tourists like to visit. You will also need to make this change in several other places.

<u>Sentence 1</u>. Change **Marie** to a male name that is popular in your new city. You will need to change this name and the possessive adjective **her** to **his** in several other places.

<u>Sentences 4 and 9.</u> Change **the Eiffel Tower** to a famous location in your new city.

<u>Sentences 5, 6, 7.</u> Change the number and the months. Use correct information about your new city.

<u>Sentences 9, 10, 11</u>. Change to information about your new city.

_____

_____

_____

_____

_____

_____

_____

_____

_____

_____

_____

For more practice with the **grammar** in this unit, go to NGL.Cengage.com/GWF.

Building Vocabulary and Spelling

Learning Words with the Sound of o in hello *

<u>o</u> = h e l l <u>o</u>   This sound is usually spelled with the letters **o, o +
consonant + final e, ow, oa, old, oe,** and another spelling.

phone   boat

ACTIVITY 15 **Which Words Do You Know?**

This list has 52 common words with the sound of <u>o</u> in hell<u>o</u>.

1. Notice the spelling patterns.

2. Check ✓ the words you know.

3. Look up new words in a dictionary. Write the meanings in your Vocabulary Notebook.

Common Words

GROUP 1:
Words spelled with **o**

☐ 1. a g o
☐ 2. a l s o
☐ 3. b o t h
☐ 4. g o
☐ 5. h e l l o
☐ 6. h o t e l
☐ 7. m o s t
☐ 8. n o b o d y
☐ 9. N o v e m b e r
☐ 10. o c e a n

☐ 11. O c t o b e r
☐ 12. o n l y
☐ 13. o p e n
☐ 14. s o

GROUP 2:
Words spelled with **o +
consonant** + final **e**

☐ 15. a l o n e
☐ 16. c l o s e
☐ 17. c l o t h e s

☐ 18. h o m e
☐ 19. h o p e
☐ 20. j o k e
☐ 21. n o s e
☐ 22. n o t e
☐ 23. p h o n e
☐ 24. s m o k e
☐ 25. s t o v e
☐ 26. t e l e p h o n e

*List is from: Spelling Vocabulary List © 2013 Keith Folse

GROUP 3:
Words that end in **ow**

- ☐ 27. b e l **o w**
- ☐ 28. f o l l **o w**
- ☐ 29. g r **o w**
- ☐ 30. k n **o w**
- ☐ 31. l **o w**
- ☐ 32. **o w** n
- ☐ 33. s h **o w**
- ☐ 34. s l **o w**
- ☐ 35. s n **o w**
- ☐ 36. t o m o r r **o w**
- ☐ 37. w i n d **o w**
- ☐ 38. y e l l **o w**

GROUP 4:
Words spelled with **oa** (in the middle of the word)

- ☐ 39. b **o a** t
- ☐ 40. c **o a** c h
- ☐ 41. c **o a** s t
- ☐ 42. c **o a** t
- ☐ 43. g **o a** l
- ☐ 44. r **o a** d
- ☐ 45. s **o a** p

GROUP 5:
Words that end in **old**

- ☐ 46. c **o l d**
- ☐ 47. g **o l d**

- ☐ 48. **o l d**
- ☐ 49. t **o l d**

GROUP 6:
Words spelled with **oe**

- ☐ 50. g **o e** s
- ☐ 51. t **o e**

GROUP 7:
Other spelling

- ☐ 52. a l t h **o u g h**

ACTIVITY 16 **Matching Words and Pictures**

Use the list in Activity 15 to write the common word that matches the picture.

1. _____

3. _____

2. _____

4. _____

5. _____   7. _____

6. _____   8. _____

ACTIVITY 17 **Spelling Words with the Sound of <u>o</u> in hell<u>o</u>**

Fill in the missing letters to spell words with the sound of <u>o</u> in hell<u>o</u>. Then copy the correct word.

1. bel __   _____   7. __ n   _____

2. kn __   _____   8. Oct __ ber   _____

3. c __ t   _____   9. h __ p __   _____

4. g __ s   _____   10. al __ n __   _____

5. __ ld   _____   11. alth __   _____

6. b __ th   _____   12 c __ st   _____

ACTIVITY 18 Writing Sentences with Vocabulary in Context

Complete each sentence with the correct word from Activity 17. Then copy the sentence with correct capital letters and punctuation.

1. the month between september and november is _____

   _____

2. how _____ are your grandparents

   _____

3. we really _____ that it does not rain tomorrow

   _____

4. a score _____ 70 on this exam is not good

   _____

5. _____ el salvador and costa rica are in central america

   _____

6. air canada 227 _____ from toronto to atlanta

   _____

7. very few people _____ the capital of malaysia

   _____

8. she passed the test _____ she did not study a lot

   _____

9. everyone wears a heavy _____ in the middle of winter

   _____

10. how many cell phones do you _____

   _____

11. kevin lives _____

   _____

12. countries such as bolivia sudan laos and mongolia do not have a _____

   _____

ACTIVITY 19 Scrambled Letters

Change the order of the letters to make a word that has the sound of **o** in hell**o**.

_____ 1. p e n o

_____ 2. e k o j

_____ 3. p h n e o t e e l

_____ 4. s l o c e

_____ 5. l o n y

_____ 6. c c o a h

_____ 7. w o l s

_____ 8. m t o s

_____ 9. y e k b a o r d

_____ 10. o s

_____ 11. s o n e

_____ 12. o g a

_____ 13. h o w s

_____ 14. n o y d o b

CD 2, Track 4 ◀)) **ACTIVITY 20 Spelling Practice**

Write the word that you hear. You will hear each word two times.

1. _____

2. _____

3. _____

4. _____

5. _____

6. _____

7. _____

8. _____

9. _____

10. _____

11. _____

12. _____

13. _____

14. _____

15. _____

ACTIVITY 21 Spelling Review: Which Word Is Correct?

This review covers the different ways of spelling **o** in hell**o** in this unit. Read each pair of words. Circle the word that is spelled correctly.

	A	B		A	B
1.	oshun	ocean	11.	tomorrow	tomorow
2.	ownly	only	12.	gole	goal
3.	below	beloe	13.	coald	cold
4.	folow	follow	14.	alown	alone
5.	know	knoe	15.	clothes	closse
6.	also	alsow	16.	joke	joake
7.	ago	agoa	17.	smoughk	smoke
8.	helo	hello	18.	althow	although
9.	own	oun	19.	sough	so
10.	slowe	slow	20.	goes	gose

Read the four words in each row from Units 1–9. Underline the word that is spelled correctly.

	A	B	C	D
1.	bothe	bouth	both	bouthe
2.	moni	muney	mney	money
3.	jome	ome	home	phome
4.	usually	yusually	uselly	usualy
5.	soap	sope	soop	sowp
6.	most	moast	mowst	moest
7.	gaym	gaim	game	guame
8.	althoh	althow	althoe	although
9.	number	nimbr	nummber	nombour
10.	oppen	open	oben	obben
11.	buthir	boter	boather	bother
12.	nobember	Nobember	november	November
13.	belo	below	billew	beloe
14.	tomorrow	tomorow	tommorow	tommorrow
15.	trabel	truvel	travel	trubel
16.	imbossible	impossible	imposibl	empossible
17.	encide	inseed	incide	inside
18.	goale	gole	gol	goal
19.	necesary	necessary	nessesery	nessesary
20.	kno	knoe	knou	know

💻 For more practice with the **spelling and vocabulary** in this unit, go to NGL.Cengage.com/GWF.

Original Student Writing

Writing Your Ideas in Sentences or a Paragraph

Write eight to twelve sentences on your own paper. Imagine that you live in a city that millions of tourists visit each year. Write about your city. What do tourists come to see there? When do they come there? What advice can you give them about things to see and do in that city? Use prepositions of place and time.

For help, you can follow the examples in Activity 13 (page 171) and Activity 14 (page 172).
(For more information about writing a paragraph, go to Appendix 4.)

Peer Editing

Exchange papers from the above activity. Read your partner's sentences.
Then use Peer Editing Sheet 9 to make comments about the writing. Go to NGL.Cengage.com/GWF. There is a sample in Appendix 3.

For more practice with the **writing** in this unit, go to NGL.Cengage.com/GWF.

Building Bigger Sentences with Coordinating Conjunctions: *and, but, so*

Elephant orphans and their caregivers form great friendships in Nairobi National Park, Kenya.

OBJECTIVES **Grammar:** To learn about coordinating conjunctions **and**, **but**, **so**
Vocabulary and Spelling: To study common words with the sound of **u** in sch**oo**l
Writing: To write about a job or hobby

Can you write about someone's job or hobby?

*I choose the two pairs of blue shoes, **but** you can choose a different pair.*

Coordinating Conjunctions: <u>and</u>, <u>but</u>, <u>so</u>

✓ The **conjunctions and, but, so** can connect two clauses. (A clause has one subject-verb combination.)

✓ The words **and, but, so** are very common conjunctions. They are called **coordinating conjunctions** because they connect two equal parts to make a compound sentence.

Using <u>and</u> in Your Writing

✓ The word **and** is used when you want to give extra information.

✓ You use a comma before **and** when there are two clauses in the sentence.

✓ You do not use a comma with **and** when there are only two nouns, two verbs, or two adjectives.

✓ Do not write a sentence that begins with **and**.

Commas with <u>and</u>		
Example	**Explanation**	
Peru is in South America, **and** it has many high mountains.	Peru is …, **and** it has …	comma between two clauses: subject + verb, **and** subject + verb
Peru is in South America **and** has many high mountains.	Peru is … **and** has …	no comma: subject + verb **and** verb
Peru **and** Ecuador are in South America.	Peru **and** Ecuador	no comma: noun **and** noun (2 items in a list)
Peru, Ecuador, **and** Brazil are in South America.	Peru, Ecuador, **and** Brazil	commas with 3 items in a list: noun, noun, **and** noun

ACTIVITY 1 **Using Commas with and**

Add a comma in the box if it is necessary. On the line, write YES or NO and explain why you need or do not need a comma.

1. My name has five letters ▢, and your name also has five letters.   *YES – 2 clauses*

2. Our favorite teachers are Mr. Foley ▢ and Mr. Wilson.   *NO – 2 nouns*

3. Apple pie is very sweet ▢ and it is my favorite dessert.   _____

4. China is a big country ▢ and it has many people.   _____

5. China is a big country ▢ and has many people.   _____

6. Becky ▢ and Sue are classmates ▢ and they live on the same street.   _____

7. The colors of the American flag are red ▢ white ▢ and blue.   _____

8. My first name has five letters ▢ and my last name also has five letters.   _____

9. Ten people work in my office ▢ and four of them are from Alaska.   _____

10. I like basketball very much ▢ and play it almost every weekend.   _____

11. I like basketball very much ▢ and I play it almost every weekend.   _____

12. Our favorite food is fish ▢ and we eat it three times a week.   _____

ACTIVITY 2 **Writing Compound Sentences with and**

Combine the two sentences to make a compound sentence with **and**. Use pronouns to avoid repeating a noun. Be sure to use a comma between the two clauses.

1. India is a large country. India has many people.

   India is a large country, and it has many people.

2. You add a little milk to your coffee. Then you drink your coffee.

   _____

3. That book has two hundred pages. That book costs twenty-two dollars.

   _____

4. Karen is from the United States. She lives in Michigan.

   _____

5. Bob and Sue are married. Bob and Sue have three children.

   _____

6. Minnesota is next to Canada. Minnesota has many lakes.

_____

7. A cheeseburger is delicious. A cheeseburger does not cost much.

_____

8. A giraffe has four long legs. A giraffe can run really fast.

_____

Using **but** in Your Writing

✓ The word **but** is used when you want to give different or opposite information.

✓ You use a comma before **but** when there are two clauses in the sentence.

✓ You do not use a comma with **but** when there is only one clause in the sentence.

✓ Do not write a sentence that begins with **but.**

Commas with <u>but</u>		
Examples	**Explanations**	
Frankfurt is a large city, **but** it is not the capital of Germany.	Frankfurt is … , **but** it is not …	comma between two clauses: subject + verb, **but** subject + verb
The weather in January is sunny **but** cold.	sunny **but** cold	no comma if there is one clause: adjective **but** adjective

ACTIVITY 3 Writing Compound Sentences with **but**

Combine the two sentences with **but**. Be sure to use a comma between the two clauses.

1. English has 26 letters. Arabic has 28 letters.

   English has 26 letters, but Arabic has 28 letters.

2. I love cheese. My brother loves vegetables.

_____

3. Marcos is from Mexico. Claudio is from Argentina.

_____

4. Shanghai is the largest city in China. Beijing is the capital.

_____

5. July has 31 days. June has 30 days.

_____

6. Wei is from China. Cho Hee is from Korea.

_____

7. Bolivia does not have a seacoast. Chile has a very long one.

_____

8. The number **two** is even. The number **nine** is odd.

_____

Using <u>so</u> in Your Writing

✓ The word **so** as a connector has two different meanings.

✓ Meaning 1: **My parents have brown eyes, so I have brown eyes.**
   As a coordinating conjunction, **so** means "and the result is" or "therefore." In this case, you use a comma before **so**.

✓ Meaning 2: **I need better English so I can get a good job in the future.**
   When **so** means "in order to" or "the purpose is," you do not use a comma. With this meaning, **so** is not a coordinating conjunction.

✓ Do not write a sentence that begins with **so** as a connector.

Commas with <u>so</u>

Examples	Explanations	
My parents have brown eyes, **so** I have brown eyes.	My parents have … , **so** I have …	Meaning 1. Use a comma. (**so** means "the result is" or "therefore")
I need better English **so** I can get a good job in the future.	I need … **so** I can …	Meaning 2. Do not use a comma. (**so** means "in order to" or "the purpose is")

ACTIVITY 4 **Writing Compound Sentences with <u>so</u> (Meaning 1)**

Combine the two sentences with **so**. Use pronouns to avoid repeating a noun. Use a comma between the two clauses.

1. Luke has a car. Luke does not take a bus to school.

   Luke has a car, so he does not take a bus to school. _____

   _____

2. Each shirt is $50. Two shirts are $100.

   _____

   _____

3. I am a vegetarian. I do not eat hot dogs.

   _____

   _____

4. It will rain later today. You need an umbrella.

_____

_____

5. My computer is broken. I can not check my e-mail.

_____

_____

6. The weather in Florida is very hot in July. That is not a good time to visit the state.

_____

_____

7. The weather in Toronto in January is cold. You need a heavy coat.

_____

_____

8. That soup has pork. I can not eat that soup.

_____

_____

9. The word **on** has more than 20 meanings. The word **on** is difficult to learn well.

_____

_____

10. My sister runs five miles every day. My sister is in good shape.

_____

_____

Combine the two sentences with **so**. Use pronouns to avoid repeating a noun. Do not use a comma between the two clauses.

1. Students wake up early. Students can get to class on time.

   Students wake up early so they can get to class on time.

2. Please study tonight. You will do well on tomorrow's test.

3. My mom adds a lot of onions to the rice. The rice will taste better.

4. You need to wear a coat. You will not be cold.

5. The best students ask questions. The best students can understand everything well.

6. I always use a pencil in math class. I can change my answers easily.

Common Student Mistakes

Student Mistake **X**	Problem	Correct Example **✓**
Five is an odd **number but** six is an even number.	comma missing	Five is an odd number, but six is an even number.
I like tea, **so** I hate coffee.	wrong connector	I like tea, **but** I hate coffee. Or: I like tea, **and** I hate coffee.
Costa Rica is in Central America. **And** Peru is in South America.	beginning a sentence with a connector	Costa Rica is in Central America, **and** Peru is in South America.

Unscrambling Clauses to Make Compound Sentences with <u>**and**</u>**,** <u>**but**</u>**,** <u>**so**</u>

You will see two groups of words and a conjunction. Change the order of the words to write a correct English sentence with the conjunction. Be careful with capital letters, commas, and end punctuation.

1. A. cook a mother very my is good

   B. not make can pizza she

   conjunction: **but**

   My mother is a very good cook , but she can not make pizza .

2. A. my are from cousins France

   B. French speak they

   conjunction: **so**

3. A. swim day my every friends

   B. they good swimmers are very

   conjunction: **so**

4. A. much we India very like

   B. we plan to go there next month

   conjunction: **and**

5. A. math books table are the on the

   B. books are on the the science desk

   conjunction: **and**

6. A. Michael on vacation and Rob are

B. one is at no their house

conjunction: **so**

_____

_____

7. A. my easy math class is

B. are difficult my classes English and Arabic

conjunction: **but**

_____

_____

8. A. light breakfast my father eats a

B. lunch he salad for eats

conjunction: **and**

_____

_____

ACTIVITY 7 **Scrambled Sentences**

Change the order of the words to write a correct sentence. Be careful with spelling, capital letters, punctuation, and word order. (Hint: Five sentences need commas.)

Visiting the Zoo

1. children so to go to the zoo they love love animals

_____

2. the animals zoo kinds has many different of

_____

3. some really big animals are but small others are

_____

4. elephants and are big animals giraffes camels

_____

5. monkeys are animals small and penguins

_____

6. my they are favorite like leopards so animal at the zoo i

_____

7. beautiful leopards really fast are can run and they

_____

8. and sister likes gazelles my pandas

_____

ACTIVITY 8 **Scrambled Sentences with <u>and</u>, <u>but</u>, <u>so</u>**

Change the order of the words to write a correct English sentence. Sometimes more than one answer is possible. Be careful with capital letters, punctuation, and word order.

1. small big libya panama is is a a but country country
Panama is a small country, but Libya is a big country.

_____

_____

2. but wei faisal are and and amani ming china from dubai are from

_____

_____

3. my with so i will mr at 8:45 meeting currier is 9 at o'clock arrive

_____

_____

4. is the brazil not city sao paolo is the largest capital but it in

_____

_____

5. she likes it a new car very Elena has and much

_____

_____

6. canada not have a is but does large large a very country it population

_____

_____

7. thai read this speaks message thai help you phatra so she can

_____

_____

8. but a it is fruit sweet not a tomato is

_____

_____

ACTIVITY 9 **Finding and Correcting 10 Mistakes**

Circle the ten mistakes. Then write the sentences correctly. The number in parentheses ( ) is the number of mistakes in that sentence. Be ready to explain your answers.

Children's Day in Japan

1. Children's Day is a holiday very special in Japan. (1)

_____

2. People in Japan celebrate Children's Day on fifth day of fifth month, the date is easy to remember. (3)

_____

3. On this day, you can to see many colorful cloth fish flying in the air. (1)

_____

4. When the wind blow, the fish seem to be swimming in very fast river. (2)

_____

5. If these fish are strong, they will reach their home and they can be happy, and successful. (2)

_____

6. On this day Japanese parents hope their children will be strong like these fish. (1)

_____

CD 2,
Track 5 •)) **ACTIVITY 10** **Dictation**

You will hear six sentences three times. Listen carefully and write the six sentences. The number in parentheses ( ) is the number of words. Be careful with capital letters and end punctuation.

1. _____ (9)

2. _____ (11)

3. _____ (10)

4. _____ (11)

5. _____ (8)

6. _____ (10)

Read the sentences in the paragraph very carefully. Fill in the missing words from the word bank.
Circle the 12 letters that need to be capital letters. Then copy the paragraph on your own paper.

walks	break	information	at	finishes	future
works	blocks	excellent	a lot	trips	company

My Brother John

1 this _____ is about my brother john. **2** john has an _____ job.

3 john likes it _____ . **4** john _____ in the travel office of

a large _____ . **5** his job is to plan _____ for people. **6** john lives

only four _____ from his office. **7** he _____ to work every day.

8 he starts work _____ 9 a.m. **9** he _____ work at 5 p.m.

10 he takes a _____ for lunch from 12:30 to 1:15. **11** i hope to have a great job like this

in the _____ .

ACTIVITY 12 **Guided Writing: Making Changes in Model Writing**

Write the paragraph from Activity 11 again, but make the changes listed below and all other necessary changes.

Sentence 1. Change **brother** to **cousin.**

Sentence 2 and 3. Combine these two sentences with **and.**

Sentence 6. Change **only** to **just.**

Sentences 6 and 7. Combine these two sentences with **so.**

Sentences 8 and 9. Combine these two sentences with **and.**

Sentence 10. Add the adjective **short** in the correct place.

Sentence 11. Change **in the future** to **one day.**

_____

_____

_____

_____

_____

_____

_____

_____

_____

_____

_____

_____

For more practice with the **grammar** in this unit, go to NGL.Cengage.com/GWF.

Building Vocabulary and Spelling

Learning Words with the Sound of u in school *

u = s c h **oo** l   This sound is usually spelled with the letters **oo, ue, u** + consonant + final **e, ew, ou, o, ui, u,** and others.

s c h **oo** l

b l **u** e

ACTIVITY 13 **Which Words Do You Know?**

This list has 42 common words with the sound of **u** in sch**oo**l.

1. Notice the spelling patterns.

2. Check ✓ the words you know.

3. Look up new words in a dictionary. Write the meanings in your Vocabulary Notebook.

Common Words

GROUP 1:
Words spelled with **oo**

- ☐ 1. c h o o s e
- ☐ 2. c o o l
- ☐ 3. f o o d
- ☐ 4. n o o n
- ☐ 5. p o o l
- ☐ 6. p o o r
- ☐ 7. r o o m
- ☐ 8. s c h o o l
- ☐ 9. s o o n
- ☐ 10. s p o o n
- ☐ 11. t o o
- ☐ 12. t o o t h
- ☐ 13. z o o

GROUP 2:
Words spelled with **ue**

- ☐ 14. b l u e
- ☐ 15. t r u e
- ☐ 16. T u e s d a y

GROUP 3:
Words spelled with **u** + consonant + final **e**

- ☐ 17. i n c l u d e
- ☐ 18. J u n e
- ☐ 19. r u l e

GROUP 4:
Words spelled with **ew**

- ☐ 20. a f e w
- ☐ 21. k n e w

*List is from: Spelling Vocabulary List © 2013 Keith Folse

☐ 22. n e w
☐ 23. n e w s
☐ 24. n e w s p a p e r

GROUP 5:
Words spelled with **ou**

☐ 25. g r **o u** p
☐ 26. s **o u** p
☐ 27. y **o u**

GROUP 6:
Words spelled with **o** (at the end of the word)

☐ 28. d **o**
☐ 29. t **o**
☐ 30. t w **o**
☐ 31. w h **o**

GROUP 7:
Words spelled with **ui**

☐ 32. f r **u i** t
☐ 33. j **u i** c e
☐ 34. s **u i** t c a s e

GROUP 8:
Words spelled with **u** and pronounced **yu**

☐ 35. c o m p **u** t e r
☐ 36. c o n f **u** s e d
☐ 37. **u** s e
☐ 38. m **u** s i c

GROUP 9:
Other spellings

☐ 39. s h **o e**
☐ 40. s t **u** d e n t
☐ 41. w h **o**'s
☐ 42. w h **o** s e

ACTIVITY 14 **Matching Words and Pictures**

Use the list in Activity 13 to write the common word that matches the picture.

1. _____

2. _____

3. _____

4. _____

5. _____   7. _____

6. _____   8. _____

ACTIVITY 15 **Spelling Words with the Sound of <u>u</u> in sch<u>oo</u>l**

Fill in the missing letters to spell words with the sound of <u>**u**</u> in sch<u>**oo**</u>l. Then copy the correct word.

1. wh __   _____   7. incl __ d __   _____

2. r __ l __   _____   8. T __ sday   _____

3. kn   _____   9. n __   _____

4. f __   _____   10. n __ s   _____

5. t __   _____   11. n __ n   _____

6. gr __ p   _____   12. tr __   _____

ACTIVITY 16 Writing Sentences with Vocabulary in Context

Complete each sentence with the correct words from Activity 15. Then copy the sentence with correct capital letters, commas, and end punctuation.

1. the day after monday is ....

_____

2. .... is the teacher for that .... of students

_____

3. does your school have a .... about coming to class on time

_____

4. there are a .... books on the table but they are not ....

_____

5. a bill in a restaurant does not usually .... a tip

_____

6. jonathan can speak chinese and he can write it ....

_____

7. sara .... all the answers on the test yesterday so her score was 100

_____

8. the opposite of false is ....

_____

9. did you hear the international .... program at .... yesterday

_____

ACTIVITY 17 Scrambled Letters

Change the order of the letters to write a word that has the sound of **u** in sch**oo**l.

_____ 1. o n o n   _____ 8. o n o s

_____ 2. c l i n u d e   _____ 9. d T u s a y e

_____ 3. n w e k   _____ 10. o t

_____ 4. o h t o t   _____ 11. o w t

_____ 5. c s a e s u i t   _____ 12. o o t

_____ 6. o o s h c e   _____ 13. t r u i f

_____ 7. f s d c o n u e   _____ 14. d o f o

ACTIVITY 18 Spelling Practice

Write the word that you hear. You will hear each word two times.

1. _____   6. _____   11. _____

2. _____   7. _____   12. _____

3. _____   8. _____   13. _____

4. _____   9. _____   14. _____

5. _____   10. _____   15. _____

ACTIVITY 19 Spelling Review: Which Word Is Correct?

This review covers the different ways of spelling **u** in sch**oo**l in this unit. Read each pair of words. Circle the word that is spelled correctly.

	A	B		A	B
1.	Joon	June	11.	choose	chuse
2.	soap	soup	12.	joos	juice
3.	schul	school	13.	spoon	spune
4.	fruit	froot	14.	tru	true
5.	shoe	shu	15.	nun	noon
6.	blu	blue	16.	inclood	include
7.	Tuesday	Tusday	17.	do	du
8.	foud	food	18.	you	yu
9.	compoter	computer	19.	roule	rule
10.	noos	news	20.	muisic	music

Read the four words in each row from Units 1–10. Underline the word that is spelled correctly.

	A	B	C	D
1.	scholl	school	schul	schule
2.	famos	famoso	femous	famous
3.	stret	estret	street	streat
4.	usually	usally	usully	usualy
5.	spon	spoon	spune	spoun
6.	bole	bowl	poul	powl
7.	shees	chees	sheese	cheese
8.	doctor	doctr	dactor	docter
9.	fainli	finali	finally	fainally
10.	Chainese	Chinese	Chineese	Chinees
11.	pipel	people	peeple	bebel
12.	Inglesh	Anglesh	English	Englis
13.	languaje	language	lenguaje	lenjuge
14.	classroom	classroon	clasroum	classroum
15.	frenly	frenli	frendly	friendly
16.	trebel	troble	truble	trouble
17.	practese	practes	practice	proctice
18.	estudent	estuden	studen	student
19.	imformation	imformetion	information	informetion
20.	reali	realy	really	realli

🖥 For more practice with the **spelling and vocaublary** in this unit, go to NGL.Cengage.com/GWF.

Original Student Writing

Writing Your Ideas in Sentences or a Paragraph

Write six to twelve sentences on your own paper. Write about a job or hobby that a family member or friend has. The job can be very good, very bad, or very interesting. Use the coordinating conjunctions **and, but, so**.

For help, you can follow the examples in Activity 11 (page 193) and Activity 12 (page 194). (For more information about writing a paragraph, go to Appendix 4.)

Peer Editing

Exchange papers from the above activity. Read your partner's sentences.

Then use Peer Editing Sheet 10 to make comments about the writing. Go to NGL.Cengage.com/GWF. There is a sample in Appendix 3.

For more practice with the **writing** in this unit, go to NGL.Cengage.com/GWF.

Verbs: Simple Past Tense

An Indian bride and groom held hands on their wedding day.

OBJECTIVES **Grammar:** To learn about simple past tense
Vocabulary and Spelling: To study common words with the sound of <u>aw</u> in <u>straw</u>
Writing: To write about one important event that happened in the past

Can you write about one important event in the past?

Grammar for Writing

I **visited** the Vietnam Veterans Memorial Wall.

Simple Past Tense

✓ In **simple past tense**, regular verbs end in **–ed: need → needed**

✓ In simple past tense, irregular verbs change in different ways: **go → went**

✓ In simple past tense, each verb has only one form, so you use **needed** or **went** after all subjects.

✓ Three common time phrases for simple past tense include **yesterday, last _____**, and **_____ ago**.

> We **needed** more gas for our car **yesterday**, so we **went** to the gas station.
>
> I **did** my homework **last** night.
>
> She **arrived** here two weeks **ago**.

Regular Verbs in Simple Past Tense

Study this chart of regular verbs.

	want	look	play	include
Singular	I **wanted**	I **looked**	I **played**	I **included**
	you **wanted**	you **looked**	you **played**	you **included**
	he **wanted**	he **looked**	he **played**	he **included**
	she **wanted**	she **looked**	she **played**	she **included**
	it **wanted**	it **looked**	it **played**	it **included**
Plural	we **wanted**	we **looked**	we **played**	we **included**
	you **wanted**	you **looked**	you **played**	you **included**
	they **wanted**	they **looked**	they **played**	they **included**

✓ Most English verbs (99.9 percent) are regular verbs that add **–ed** for simple past tense:
want → wanted

✓ For verbs that end in **–e** already, add only **–d: include → included**

✓ For verbs that end in consonant + **y**, change the **–y** to **–i** and add **–ed: try → tried**

✓ For verbs that end in vowel + **y**, add **–ed: enjoy → enjoyed**

✓ The **–ed** ending has three pronunciations, but the spelling is always **–ed: needed** /əd/, **finished** /t/, and **played** /d/.

Single or Double Consonant?

One Syllable		Two Syllables	
+ –ed	**double consonant + –ed**	**+ –ed**	**double consonant + –ed** (when the accent is on the second syllable)
want**ed**	stop**ped**	happen**ed**	occur**red**
need**ed**	plan**ned**	open**ed**	permit**ted**
add**ed**	rob**bed**	follow**ed**	
look**ed**		return**ed**	

✓ For one-syllable verbs that end in consonant + vowel + consonant (CVC), double the last letter before adding **–ed**.

✓ For two-syllable verbs that end in consonant + vowel + consonant (CVC), double the last letter before adding **–ed** only if the pronunciation stress is on the second syllable.

ACTIVITY 1 **Practicing the 29 Most Common Regular Past Tense Verbs in Writing***

Write the past tense of the 29 most common verbs in English writing.

present	past		present	past
1. want	_____		11. include	_____
2. ask	_____		12. receive	_____
3. start	_____		13. decide	_____
4. seem	_____		14. try	_____
5. use	_____		15. call	_____
6. show	_____		16. play	_____
7. report	_____		17. look	_____
8. turn	_____		18. appear	_____
9. die	_____		19. help	_____
10. work	_____		20. move	_____

*Source: Corpus of Contemporary American English

present	past		present	past
21. happen	_____		**26.** live	_____
22. add	_____		**27.** create	_____
23. learn	_____		**28.** believe	_____
24. continue	_____		**29.** suggest	_____
25. open	_____			

ACTIVITY 2 **Writing Sentences with Regular Past Tense Verbs**

Use one word from each of the four groups to write five new sentences. Be careful with capital letters, verb form (–ed), and periods. Follow the example.

Subject	Verb	Object	Time
he	watch	a football game	last night
we	play	a DVD	yesterday
they	enjoy	a basketball game	three days ago

Example: _We watched a DVD last night ._____

1. _____

2. _____

3. _____

4. _____

5. _____

ACTIVITY 3 **PAIR WORK: Who Has the Most Sentences That Are Different?**

Work with another student. Compare your sentences from Activity 2. You receive one point for each sentence that your partner does not have.

1ˢᵗ time: _____ / 5 points possible

When you finish, work with another student. Each different sentence receives one point.

2ⁿᵈ time: _____ / 5 points possible

Your total: _____ / 10 points possible

Irregular Verbs in Simple Past Tense

Study this chart of irregular verbs in simple past tense.

	be	have	do	take	think
Singular	I was you were he was she was it was	I had you had he had she had it had	I did you did he did she did it did	I took you took he took she took it took	I thought you thought he thought she thought (Note: It is not usually used with **thought**.)
Plural	we were you were they were	we had you had they had	we did you did they did	we took you took they took	we thought you thought they thought

✓ English has thousands of verbs, but only a very small number of useful verbs — perhaps 150 — are **irregular.**

✓ In English, these irregular verbs are used very often. In fact, the top ten verbs in English are all irregular: **was/were, had, did, said, came, got, went, made, took, thought.**

✓ Many verbs for daily activities are irregular: **eat → ate; drink → drank; speak → spoke; wake → woke.**

✓ For the verb **be**, you use **was** after **I, he, she, it**. Use **were** after **you, we,** and **they**. All other verbs have only one form for all subjects: **I went / she went / they went.**

ACTIVITY 4 **Practicing the 30 Most Common Irregular Past Tense Verbs in Writing***

Write the present tense of these irregular verbs that are in simple past tense.

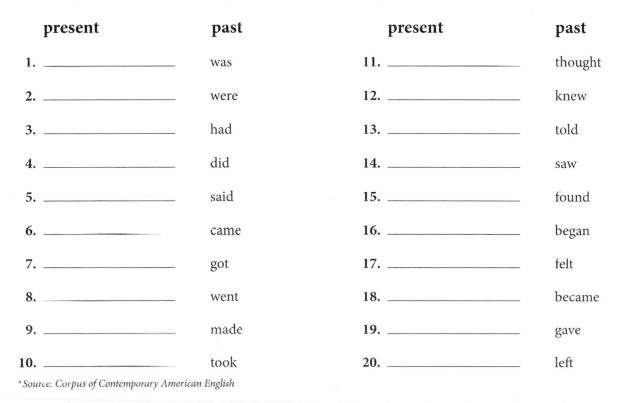

	present	past		present	past
1.	_____	was	11.	_____	thought
2.	_____	were	12.	_____	knew
3.	_____	had	13.	_____	told
4.	_____	did	14.	_____	saw
5.	_____	said	15.	_____	found
6.	_____	came	16.	_____	began
7.	_____	got	17.	_____	felt
8.	_____	went	18.	_____	became
9.	_____	made	19.	_____	gave
10.	_____	took	20.	_____	left

* *Source: Corpus of Contemporary American English*

present	past	present	past
21. _____	wrote	26. _____	ran
22. _____	heard	27. _____	kept
23. _____	sat	28. _____	held
24. _____	stood	29. _____	brought
25. _____	put	30. _____	lost

ACTIVITY 5 Writing Sentences with Irregular Past Tense Verbs

Answer each question with a complete sentence. Pay attention to spelling, capital letters, and periods. Follow the example. When you finish, work with another student to compare answers.

Example: What time did you come to class today?

I came to class at 9 o'clock. _____

1. What time did you get up this morning?

   _____

2. Where did you go last summer?

   _____

3. When were you born?

   _____

4. How much pasta did you eat last week?

   _____

5. When did you do your homework?

   _____

6. How many pets did you have ten years ago?

   _____

7. Where did you buy your shoes?

   _____

8. How many e-mails did you write last month?

   _____

Common Student Mistakes

Student Mistake X	Problem	Correct Example ✓
Mizumi an e-mail to her parents.	verb missing	Mizumi **wrote** an e-mail to her parents.
We **live** in London in 2010	past tense missing	We **lived** in London in 2010.
John and I **goed** to Brazil in 2005.	past tense form	John and I **went** to Brazil in 2005.
I **was** took Bus 87 yesterday.	extra verb	I **took** Bus 87 yesterday.

ACTIVITY 6 **Correcting Mistakes with Past Tense Verbs in Context**

Each sentence has a verb mistake. Correct the mistake. Then write each sentence again, but pay attention to capital letters, commas, and periods.

Some Strong Medicine

1. i catch a cold two or three days ago

_____

2. last night i feel a little sick

_____

3. i was took two aspirins and then i went to bed

_____

4. i usually got up at 8 o'clock but today i got up at 6:30

_____

5. i were very sick so i went to see my doctor

_____

6. he sayed i had a very high fever

_____

7. he was told me to go home and rest

_____

8. on the way home, i stopped at the drugstore

_____

9. i was buy some stronger medicine

_____

10. maybe i will felt better tomorrow

_____

Negative of Verbs in Simple Past Tense

Making a negative is very easy. You use the special helping verb **did** before the word **not**: **did not + verb**. (The verb should be the simple or base form.)

✓ Use **did not** with all verbs (except **was, were, could, would**).

✓ With **was, were, could,** and **would,** just add **not** after the word.

✓ You can also use a short form (called a **contraction**) in speaking and in friendly writing such as e-mail: **didn't.** Do not use contractions in formal writing.

	be	have	do	take
Singular	I was **not**	I **did not** have	I **did not** do	I **did not** take
	you **were not**	you **did not** have	you **did not** do	you **did not** take
	he was **not**	he **did not** have	he **did not** do	he **did not** take
	she **was not**	she **did not** have	she **did not** do	she **did not** take
	it **was not**	it **did not** have	it **did not** do	it **did not** take
Plural	we **were not**	we **did not** have	we **did not** do	we **did not** take
	you **were not**	you **did not** have	you **did not** do	you **did not** take
	they **were not**	they **did not** have	they **did not** do	they **did not** take

Common Student Mistakes

Student Mistake **X**	Problem	Correct Example **✓**
Andrea **no lived** in Korea in 2011.	negative form	Andrea **did not live** in Korea in 2011.
We **do not arrived** late.	forms of helping verb and main verb	We **did not arrive** late.
I did not **took** the bus yesterday.	form of main verb	I did not **take** the bus yesterday.
Norah **was** not wake up at 7 this morning.	helping verb	Norah **did** not wake up at 7 this morning.

ACTIVITY 7 **Scrambled Sentences**

Change the order of the words to write a correct sentence. Be careful with spelling, capital letters, punctuation, and word order.

Omar's Difficult Final Test

1. english at omar college studies lincoln

   _____

2. reading yesterday final class the was for test his

   _____

3. difficult was test very the

_____

4. exam hours and was not two the took finish short, to it omar it

_____

5. short have did questions not the any test

_____

6. three the omar questions not to know did answers

_____

7. minutes his ago he a score out few found

_____

8. for good 81 a he score of that test, got difficult

_____

ACTIVITY 8 **Finding and Correcting 10 Mistakes**

Circle the ten mistakes. Then write the sentences correctly. The number in parentheses ( ) is the number of mistakes in that sentence. Be ready to explain your answers.

A Late Flight

1. My husband and I live in very small town in Texas. (1)

_____

2. My mother come to visit us today, so we go to the airport to pick her up. (2)

_____

3. Unfortunately, his flight did not arrived on time. (2)

_____

4. The weather was very bad, almost all the flights tonight arrive late. (2)

_____

5. My mother's flight was about two hour late. (1)

_____

6. We finally were got home midnight before. (2)

_____

ACTIVITY 9 **Dictation**

You will hear six sentence three times. Listen carefully and write the six sentences. The number in parentheses ( ) is the number of words in the sentence. Be careful with capital letters and end punctuation.

1. _____ (8)

2. _____ (9)

3. _____ (8)

4. _____ (9)

5. _____ (6)

6. _____ (9)

ACTIVITY 10 **Practicing Grammar and Vocabulary in Model Writing**

Read the sentences in the paragraph very carefully. Fill in the missing words from the word bank. Circle the 19 letters that need to be capital letters. Then copy the paragraph on your own paper.

ingredients	covers	sauce	for	almost
daughter	pieces	juicy	in	food

A Special Event

1 my _____ laura loves italian food, and she knows how to cook very well.

2 she cooks a delicious italian chicken dish _____ every week. **3** she buys fresh

_____. **4** she cuts up onions, peppers, and garlic. **5** she fries them with some olive oil

_____ a large pan. **6** she cuts the chicken into small _____.

7 she puts a little flour on the chicken pieces. **8** she adds _____ to the fried vegetables.

9 she cooks everything for about ten minutes. **10** then she cuts up two large, _____

tomatoes and adds them to the pan. **11** laura also adds salt, pepper, and basil. **12** she does not add a lot.

13 she _____ the pan with a lid and lets everything cook _____

twenty minutes. **14** she tastes the _____ one last time to check the flavor.

15 a meal from laura is always a special event.

Write the paragraph from Activity 10 again, but make your new sentences about yesterday's dinner. Make the changes listed below and all other necessary changes.

<u>Sentence 2</u>. Change **almost every week** to **yesterday.** Change the verb tense as necessary in all the sentences.

<u>Sentences 4 and 5</u>. Combine these two sentences with **and.**

<u>Sentences 6, 7, and 8</u>. Combine these three sentences with **and**. In sentence 7, use a pronoun for **pieces.**

<u>Sentences 11 and 12</u>. Combine these two sentences with **but.**

<u>Sentences 13, 14, and 15</u>. Make sure you use the correct verb tense.

_____

_____

_____

_____

_____

_____

_____

_____

_____

_____

_____

_____

_____

For more practice with the **grammar** in this unit, go to NGL.Cengage.com/GWF.

Building Vocabulary and Spelling

Learning Words with the Sound of aw in straw *

aw = s t r **a w**   This sound is usually spelled with the letters **aw, au, all, al, ough,** and **ong**.

s t r a w

d r a w

ACTIVITY 12 **Which Words Do You Know?**

This list has 39 words with the sound of **aw** in str**aw**.

1. Notice the spelling patterns.

2. Check ✔ the words you know.

3. Look up new words in a dictionary. Write the meanings in your Vocabulary Notebook.

Common Words

GROUP 1:
Words spelled with **aw**

☐ 1. **aw**ful
☐ 2. d r **a w**
☐ 3. d r **a w** e r
☐ 4. l **a w**
☐ 5. r **a w**
☐ 6. s **a w**
☐ 7. s t r **a w**

GROUP 2:
Words spelled with **au**

☐ 8. **Au**g u s t
☐ 9. **au**t h o r
☐ 10. **au**t o m o b i l e
☐ 11. **au**t u m n
☐ 12. c **au**g h t
☐ 13. c **au**s e
☐ 14. d **au**g h t e r

☐ 15. l **au**n d r y
☐ 16. s **au**c e
☐ 17. t **au**g h t

GROUP 3:
Words spelled with **all**

☐ 18. **all**
☐ 19. b **all**
☐ 20. c **all**

*List is from: Spelling Vocabulary List ©2013 Keith Folse

- ☐ 21. f a l l
- ☐ 22. m a l l
- ☐ 23. s m a l l
- ☐ 24. t a l l
- ☐ 25. w a l l

GROUP 4:
Words spelled with **al**

- ☐ 26. a l m o s t
- ☐ 27. a l s o
- ☐ 28. a l w a y s

- ☐ 29. s a l t
- ☐ 30. t a l k
- ☐ 31. w a l k

GROUP 5:
Words spelled with **ough**

- ☐ 32. b o u g h t
- ☐ 33. b r o u g h t
- ☐ 34. c o u g h
- ☐ 35. t h o u g h t

GROUP 6:
Words spelled with **ong**

- ☐ 36. l o n g
- ☐ 37. s o n g
- ☐ 38. s t r o n g
- ☐ 39. w r o n g

ACTIVITY 13 **Matching Words and Pictures**

Use the list in Activity 12 to write the common word that matches the picture.

1. _____

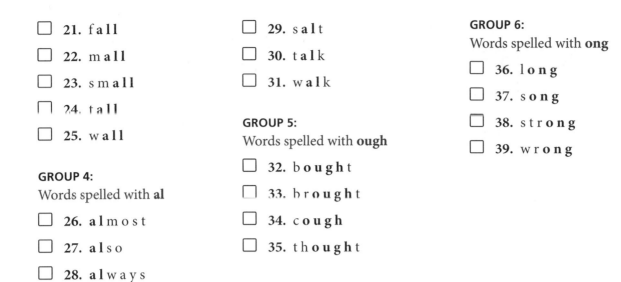

3. _____

2. _____

4. _____

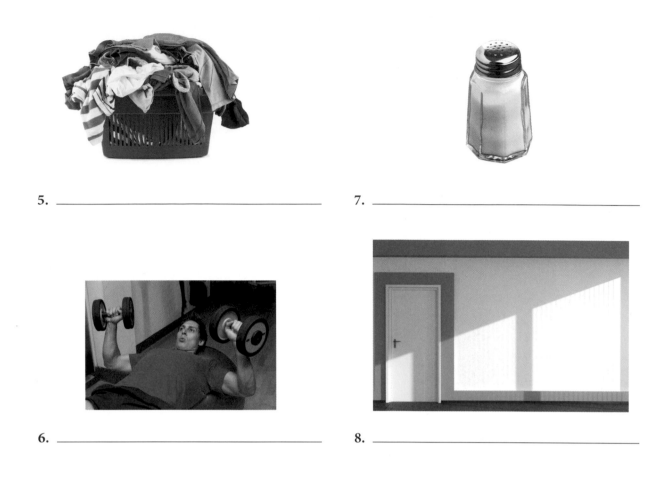

5. _____

6. _____

7. _____

8. _____

ACTIVITY 14 **Spelling Words with the Sound of _aw_ in straw**

Fill in the missing letters to spell words with the sound of __aw__ in str__aw__. Then copy the correct word.

1. __ gust   _____

2. t __ ll   _____

3. r __   _____

4. s __ ce   _____

5. wr __ ng   _____

6. __ ful   _____

7. d __ ghter   _____

8. __ lways   _____

9. th __ ght   _____

10. dr __   _____

ACTIVITY 15 **Writing Sentences with Vocabulary in Context**

Complete each sentence with the correct word from Activity 14. Then copy the sentence with correct capital letters and punctuation.

1. maria used tomato .... for her pasta dinner

_____

2. ling had only one .... answer on the test so her score was 95

_____

3. my brother is very .... but my sister and I are short

_____

4. my sister .... about the problem for a long time

_____

5. we really like tennis so we .... play tennis on monday and thursday

_____

6. the month before september is ....

_____

7. this food is .... and I cannot finish it

_____

8. my wife and I have three sons and one ....

_____

9. it is very difficult to .... human hands

_____

10. sushi uses .... fish

_____

ACTIVITY 16 **Scrambled Letters**

Change the order of the letters to write a word that has the sound of <u>aw</u> in str<u>aw</u>.

_____ 1. a t m n u u _____ 8. s t a l o m

_____ 2. e s a u c   _____ 9. w r a d

_____ 3. w l a   _____ 10. g l o n

_____ 4. l a b l   _____ 11. t t a g h u

_____ 5. a l l f   _____ 12. l a c l

_____ 6. r o h t a u _____ 13. b g h r t u o

_____ 7. s o a l   _____ 14. k l a w

CD 2, Track 8 **ACTIVITY 17** **Spelling Practice**

Write the word that you hear. You will hear each word two times.

1. _____ 6. _____ 11. _____

2. _____ 7. _____ 12. _____

3. _____ 8. _____ 13. _____

4. _____ 9. _____ 14. _____

5. _____ 10. _____ 15. _____

Spelling Review: Which Word Is Correct?

This review covers the different ways of spelling the sound of <u>aw</u> in str<u>aw</u> in this unit. Read each pair of words. Circle the word that is spelled correctly.

	A	B		A	B
1.	bot	bought	**11.**	athor	author
2.	fall	foll	**12.**	almost	allmost
3.	small	smal	**13.**	straw	straugh
4.	all	al	**14.**	solt	salt
5.	allso	also	**15.**	daughter	doughter
6.	wraung	wrong	**16.**	strang	strong
7.	sauce	sos	**17.**	draw	drau
8.	cose	cause	**18.**	caugh	cough
9.	rau	raw	**19.**	towl	tall
10.	caught	cawght	**20.**	wak	walk

ACTIVITY 19 **Cumulative Spelling Review**

Read the four words in each row from Units 1–11. Underline the word that is spelled correctly.

	A	B	C	D
1.	cought	caught	caght	caughte
2.	allmost	allmst	almust	almost
3.	practese	practes	practice	proctice
4.	doughter	doghter	dawter	daughter
5.	schooll	school	shool	shooll
6.	sonetimes	sonetines	sommetimes	sometimes
7.	imbortant	important	imbortent	importent
8.	laundy	loundy	laundry	loundry
9.	study	stady	estudy	estady
10.	future	fuetur	futur	futoore
11.	cntinue	cantinue	continue	cuntinue

	A	B	C	D
12.	smoke	smok	esmoke	esmok
13.	jus	juis	juise	juice
14.	cusent	cousin	cousine	cusin
15.	amizeng	amizing	amazing	amazeng
16.	pic	pick	bic	bick
17.	aftar	eftar	after	aftair
18.	problem	proplem	problam	proplam
19.	trable	travle	trouble	trouvle
20.	little	littil	leetil	leetle
21.	reeson	reasone	raison	reason
22.	Wendsday	Wednesday	Windsday	Wednisday
23.	famous	famos	femos	faimous
24.	usully	usualli	usuali	usually
25.	Chainese	Chinese	Chineese	Chinees

For more practice with the **spelling and vocabulary** in this unit, go to NGL.Cengage.com/GWF.

Original Student Writing

Writing Your Ideas in Sentences or a Paragraph

Write six to twelve sentences on your own paper. Write about one important event that happened in the past. Examples include a birthday, a graduation, a very happy day, or a very important event to you. Use simple past tense verbs. For help, you can follow the examples in Activity 7 (page 211), Activity 8 (page 212), or Activity 11 (page 215). (For more information about writing a paragraph, go to Appendix 4.)

Peer Editing

Exchange papers from the above activity. Read your partner's sentences.
Then use Peer Editing Sheet 11 to make comments about the writing. Go to NGL.Cengage.com/GWF.
There is a sample in Appendix 3.

For more practice with the **writing** in this unit, go to NGL.Cengage.com/GWF.

Building Bigger Sentences with Subordinating Conjunctions: *because, after, before, when, if*

When the base jumpers were ready, they jumped from the Jim Mao Tower in Shanghai, China.

OBJECTIVES **Grammar:** To learn about subordinating conjunctions
Vocabulary and Spelling: To study common words with the sound of <u>u</u> in w<u>oo</u>d
Writing: To write about an important day or time in your life

Can you write about an important day or time in your life?

Grammar for Writing

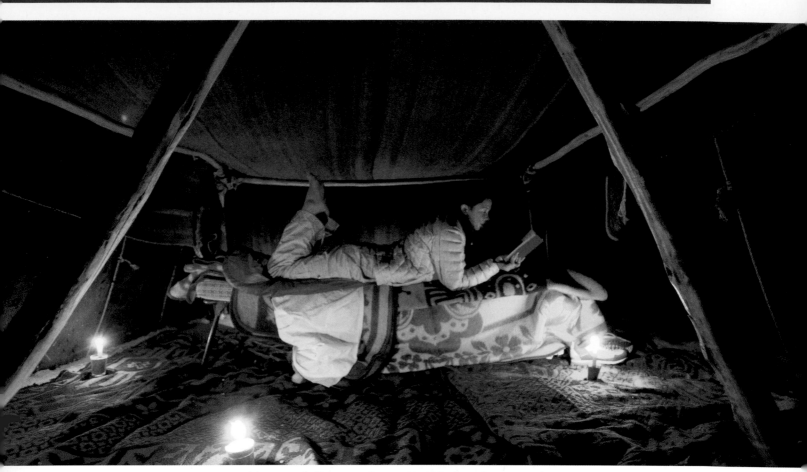

*Many people like to read a good book **before** they go to sleep.*

Subordinating Conjunctions: <u>because</u>, <u>after</u>, <u>before</u>, <u>when</u>, <u>if</u>

✓ The words **because, after, before, when,** and **if** are common conjunctions. They are very useful in good writing.

✓ These five words can connect two clauses. (A clause has a subject and a verb.)

✓ These five words connect two clauses to make a bigger sentence. The main clause (independent clause) can be a sentence all by itself.

✓ The dependent clause cannot stand by itself. The dependent clause needs the main clause to make sense. In other words, the dependent clause depends on the main clause.

Sentence	Main Clause	Dependent Clause
I failed the test **because** I did not study.	I failed the test	**because** I did not study.
Joe watches TV **after** he finishes dinner.	Joe watches TV	**after** he finishes dinner.
Many tourists need a visa **before** they can travel to the United States.	Many tourists need a visa	**before** they can travel to the United States.
People should be careful **when** they use a knife.	People should be careful	**when** they use a knife.
We will walk to class **if** the rain stops.	We will walk to class	**if** the rain stops.

Underline the main clause and put parentheses ( ) around the dependent clause.

Lim's Birthday

1. <u>I am going to bake a cake for Lim</u> (because tomorrow is his birthday).

2. I am going to make a chocolate cake because chocolate is his favorite kind of cake.

3. I need to go to the store before I can make Lim's cake.

4. I have to buy a lot of flour and sugar if I want to make a very big cake.

5. I can watch TV after I finish Lim's cake.

6. Lim is going to be so happy when he sees his birthday cake.

7. My brother will buy 26 candles for Lim's cake because Lim is going to be 26 years old.

8. My brother will put the candles on the cake when it is ready.

9. Lim's sister will sing Happy Birthday because she has a great voice.

10. Everyone will be happy if Lim is happy.

Word Order in Your Sentences

✓ The conjunctions **because, after, before, when,** and **if** often come in the middle of a sentence. The usual word order is <u>main clause</u> + <u>dependent clause</u>. The conjunction is part of the dependent clause.

Main Clause (S + V)	Dependent Clause (Conjunction + S + V)
John is hungry now	**because** <u>he</u> <u>did not eat</u> breakfast.

✓ It is also possible to begin a sentence with a dependent clause. In this case, the sentence begins with the conjunction **because, after, before, when,** or **if,** and you must use a comma after the dependent clause. The comma means the usual word order is not occurring.

✓ You do not use a comma before a dependent clause inside a sentence.

Dependent Clause (Conjunction + S + V)	Main Clause (S + V)
Because <u>John</u> <u>did not eat</u> breakfast,	he is hungry now.

✓ In a sentence with a noun and a pronoun, you use a noun the first time and a pronoun the second time. It does not matter which clause the noun or pronoun is in.

John is hungry now because **he** did not eat breakfast.

Because **John** did not eat breakfast, **he** is hungry now.

ACTIVITY 2 **Using Commas with Main and Dependent Clauses**

Underline the main clause and put parentheses ( ) around the dependent clause. Add a comma if the dependent clause comes before the main clause.

Lim's Birthday

1. (Because tomorrow is Lim's birthday), <u>I am going to bake a cake for him</u>.

2. Because chocolate is his favorite kind of cake I am going to make a chocolate cake.

3. Before I can make Lim's cake I need to go to the store.

4. I have to buy a lot of flour and sugar if I want to make a very big cake.

5. After I finish Lim's cake I can watch TV.

6. Lim is going to be so happy when he sees his birthday cake.

7. Because Lim is going to be 26 years old my brother will buy 26 candles for Lim's cake.

8. When the cake is ready my brother will put the candles on it.

9. Lim's sister will sing Happy Birthday because she has a great voice.

10. If Lim is happy his friends will be happy.

Using <u>because</u> in Your Writing

✓ The word **because** is used when you want to give a reason or explain something in the main clause.

✓ You can use **because** for the present, the past, or the future.

Time	Main Clause	Reason Clause (Dependent Clause with <u>because</u>)
present	I study every night	**because** I want to make good grades.
past	I failed the math test	**because** I did not understand the lesson.
future	I will study tonight	**because** we have a test tomorrow.

✓ When a sentence begins with a **because**-clause, you use a comma after the dependent clause.

✓ You do not use a comma if the main clause begins the sentence.

dependent clause main clause	Use a comma.
Because it was expensive, Pablo did not buy it.	The dependent clause comes first.
main clause dependent clause	Do not use a comma.
Pablo did not buy the car **because** it was expensive.	The dependent clause comes second.

ACTIVITY 3 **Using Commas with <u>because</u>**

Each pair of sentences has the same meaning. Add commas where necessary. Be ready to explain your answers.

1. a. You should wear a hat ☐ because it is sunny today.

   b. Because it is sunny today ☐ you should wear a hat.

2. a. Chinese is a difficult language for me ☐ because my language uses a different alphabet.

   b. Because my language uses a different alphabet ☐ Chinese is a difficult language for me.

3. a. It took me two weeks to read that book ☐ because it has 300 pages.

   b. Because that book has 300 pages ☐ it took me two weeks to read it.

4. a. Because Marie is from France ☐ she speaks French.

   b. Marie speaks French ☐ because she is from France.

5. a. Because it was so cold outside ☐ Ryan closed the window in his bedroom.

   b. Ryan closed the window in his bedroom ☐ because it was so cold outside.

6. a. We plan to live in Japan for one month ☐ because we want to learn Japanese.

   b. Because we want to learn Japanese ☐ we plan to live in Japan for one month.

7. a. Some people cannot eat cheese ☐ because they cannot have any milk products.

   b. Because some people cannot have any milk products ☐ they cannot eat cheese.

8. a. Giraffes are my favorite animal ☐ because they are very interesting.

   b. Because giraffes are very interesting ☐ they are my favorite animal.

ACTIVITY 4 **Writing Longer Sentences with <u>because</u>**

Combine the two sentences with **because** to make two longer sentences. Use pronouns to avoid repeating a noun. Be careful with capitalization, commas, and periods.

1. my sister will study tonight   she has a test tomorrow

   My sister will study tonight because she has a test tomorrow.

   Because my sister has a test tomorrow, she will study tonight.

2. you need an umbrella   it is raining now

3. the people understood the speaker easily   the speaker was excellent

_____

_____

4. my car is making a noise   I am taking my car to the repair shop

_____

_____

5. many irish families moved to america in the 1800s   life in ireland was difficult

_____

_____

6. the word **get** has many different meanings   the word **get** is difficult to use correctly

_____

_____

Using <u>after</u>, <u>before</u>, <u>when</u> in Your Writing

✓ The words **after, before,** and **when** are used in a time clause to explain the time relationship between the two clauses.

Conjunction	Main Clause	Time Clause (Dependent Clause with <u>after, before, when</u>)
after	I go home	**after** I finish my classes.
before	I eat breakfast	**before** I go to school.
when	I play computer games	**when** I have free time.

✓ When a sentence begins with **after, before,** or **when,** you use a comma.

✓ You do not use a comma if the main clause begins the sentence.

dependent clause main clause **Before** Pablo went to the airport, he did not call anyone.	Use a comma. The dependent clause comes first.
main clause dependent clause Pablo did not call anyone **before** he went to the airport.	Do not use a comma. The dependent clause comes second.

✓ **After** and **before** can also be prepositions. When a prepositional phrase begins a sentence, you usually use a comma.

prepositional phrase Pablo did not call anyone **before** his flight.	Do not use a comma. The prepositional phrase does not begin the sentence.
prepositional phrase **Before** his flight, Pablo did not call anyone.	Use a comma. The prepositional phrase begins the sentence.

ACTIVITY 5 Using Commas with _after_, _before_, _when_

Each pair of sentences has the same meaning. Add commas where necessary. Be ready to explain your answers.

1. a. Most children learn the names of the colors ☐ before they go to school.

   b. Before most children go to school ☐ they learn the names of the colors.

2. a. Jason went to work ☐ after he finished his breakfast.

   b. After Jason finished his breakfast ☐ he went to work.

3. a. When my father drives to work ☐ he listens to news on the radio.

   b. My father listens to news on the radio ☐ when he drives to work.

4. a. I added two cups of sugar ☐ after I added one cup of flour.

   b. After I added one cup of flour ☐ I added two cups of sugar.

5. a. When Jeff turned on the computer ☐ nothing happened.

   b. Nothing happened ☐ when Jeff turned on the computer.

6. a. My friends pushed my car ☐ when I could not start it.

   b. When I could not start my car ☐ my friends pushed it.

7. a. I wrote ten e-mails ☐ before I left the office.

   b. Before I left the office ☐ I wrote ten e-mails.

8. a. When we traveled from New York to Argentina ☐ the airline gave us dinner and breakfast.

   b. The airline gave us dinner and breakfast ☐ when we traveled from New York to Argentina.

ACTIVITY 6 Writing Two Longer Sentences with _after_, _before_, _when_

Combine the two sentences and the conjunction to make two longer sentences. Use pronouns to avoid repeating a noun. Be careful with capitalization, commas, and periods.

1. I heard your good news   I was so happy   when

   I was so happy when I heard your good news.

   When I heard your good news, I was so happy.

2. you should read the bill carefully   you pay the bill   before

3. we went to bed   we watched that long movie   after

_____

_____

4. I ate lunch   I washed my dish and put it in the cabinet   after

_____

_____

5. Natalia went to England   Natalia did not speak any English   before

_____

_____

6. my sister decided to buy those shoes   my sister saw the low price of those shoes   when

_____

_____

Using _if_ in Your Writing

✓ Sometimes the main clause shows a result, and the dependent clause gives a condition, or a limit, for that result. In this case, the word **if** is used to show this condition relationship between two clauses.

Main Clause (The Result)	Dependent Clause with _if_ (The Condition)
You cannot check your e-mail in this room	**if** the Internet does not work here.
You need six eggs	**if** you want to make a cake for ten people.
The passengers will miss their second flight	**if** their first flight arrives late.

✓ When a sentence begins with **if,** you use a comma. You do not use a comma when the main clause begins the sentence.

main clause dependent clause We will play basketball if we have extra time.	Do not use a comma. The dependent clause comes second.
dependent clause main clause If we have extra time, we will play basketball.	Use a comma. The dependent clause comes first.

ACTIVITY 7 Using Commas with _if_

Each pair of sentences has the same meaning. Add commas where necessary. Be ready to explain your answers.

   1. a. If you eat more vegetables and less red meat ☐ you will be in better health.

      b. You will be in better health ☐ if you eat more vegetables and less red meat.

2. a. The answer to this question is 116 ☐ if you multiply the two numbers.

   b. If you multiply the two numbers ☐ the answer to this question is 116.

3. a. If a storm comes near our area ☐ you should listen to the radio.

   b. You should listen to the radio ☐ if a storm comes near our area.

4. a. Linda cannot eat this soup ☐ if there is meat in it.

   b. If there is meat in this soup ☐ Linda cannot eat it.

5. a. If you have any problems ☐ you should call me immediately.

   b. You should call me immediately ☐ if you have any problems.

6. a. If the weather is cold tomorrow ☐ everyone will need a heavy sweater.

   b. Everyone will need a heavy sweater ☐ if the weather is cold tomorrow.

ACTIVITY 8 **Writing Two Longer Sentences with if**

Read the two sentences and decide which is the **if**-clause (or condition clause) and which is the main (result) clause. Combine the two sentences with **if** to make two longer sentences. Use pronouns to avoid repeating a noun. Be careful with capitalization, commas, and periods.

1. my sister studies with her friends   she has an important test

   My sister studies with her friends if she has an important test.

   If my sister has an important test, she studies with her friends.

2. you read this book   you will laugh a lot

3. Rob can fix your computer   your computer is broken

4. The lake will freeze tonight   the weather is really cold

5. Sarah travels to China on November 16   the ticket will cost $1,500

6. I do not know the meaning of a word   I look up the meaning in a dictionary

_____

_____

Common Student Mistakes

Student Mistake X	Problem	Correct Example ✓
You need a **sweater, because** the weather is cold.	comma before a dependent clause inside a sentence	You need a sweater **because** the weather is cold.
Because the weather is **cold you** need a sweater.	comma missing	Because the weather is cold**,** you need a sweater.
Because the weather is cold.	sentence fragment	**Because the weather is cold, you need a sweater.** OR **You need a sweater because the weather is cold.**

ACTIVITY 9 Correcting Fragments

The following sentences are fragments because they do not contain both a main clause and a dependent clause. Add information to make each sentence complete.

1. Because I need to learn English to get a better job.

> _I selected this school because I need to learn English to get a better job._

OR

> _Because I need to learn English to get a better job, I selected this school._

2. When I turned on the computer.

_____

3. Before everyone entered the office.

_____

4. If you work very hard this year.

_____

5. After you add the onions and the other vegetables to the pan.

_____

6. Because no one in my family speaks Spanish.

_____

7. When the weather in our area is very hot.

_____

8. Because my new phone is so hard to use.

_____

ACTIVITY 10 **Scrambled Sentences**

Change the order of the words to write a correct sentence. Be careful with spelling, capital letters, final punctuation, and word order. If there is a comma, it must stay with its word as shown. Do not add any commas.

Falling in Love with a New Pizza Restaurant

1. food is my favorite pizza

_____

2. because it pizza lot of has a i like cheese

_____

3. pizza night a went last a pizza, so eat restaurant wanted monday I to I

_____

4. was name the pizza the country restaurant of

_____

5. me about went country because a to pizza friend told it i

_____

6. I walked I had about the place when inside, a good feeling

_____

7. of restaurant looked menu had the many different kinds nice, and the pizzas

_____

8. the ten on the menu, kinds of pizza I order after I read about to decided the chicken pizza

_____

9. pizza, I was in love with this first piece of my when place tasted the I

_____

10. I recommend pizza pizza, want to if you eat a really delicious country

_____

ACTIVITY 11 **Finding and Correcting 10 Mistakes**

Circle the ten mistakes. Then write the sentences correctly. The number in parentheses ( ) is the number of mistakes in that sentence. Be ready to explain your answers.

Labneh and Provoleta

1. One of my favorite thing to eat is the cheese, and there are hundreds of different types of cheese. (2)

_____

2. When I was in Saudi Arabia, ate the labneh almost every day. (2)

_____

3. I like this creamy cheese, because it is has a good flavor and is low in calories (2)

_____

4. When were my family and I in Argentina, we ordered provoleta for dinner at least twice a week. (1)

_____

5. Argentineans grilled this thick cheese, and they use a fork and a knife to cut them just like a steak. (2)

_____

6. I like to eat all kinds of cheese, but labneh from the Saudi Arabia and provoleta from Argentina are my two favorite types of cheese. (1)

_____

_____

ACTIVITY 12 Dictation

You will hear six sentences three times. Listen carefully and write the six sentences. The number in parentheses ( ) is the number of words. Be careful with capital letters and end punctuation.

1. _____ (8)

2. _____ (9)

3. _____ (9)

4. _____ (10)

5. _____ (15)

6. _____ (12)

ACTIVITY 13 **Practicing Grammar and Vocabulary in Model Writing**

Read the sentences in the paragraph very carefully. Fill in the missing words from the word bank. Circle the 33 letters that need to be capital letters. Add commas in the correct places. Then copy the paragraph on your own paper.

received	about	for	beginning	graduated	become	wanted
immediately	when	flew	important	enjoyed	advice	forget

An Important Day in My Life

1 this story is about an _____ day in my life. **2** in may 2009,

i _____ from my university. **3** i studied education and i wanted to

_____ a teacher. **4** i _____ to teach in brazil. **5** i looked on the

internet for information _____ a job in brazil. **6** _____ i

found a really good job posting i wrote an e-mail to the school. **7** on that day, i _____

a letter that offered me that job. **8** after i got that letter i talked to my family for their

_____. **9** my parents liked this job a lot so i _____ accepted the job.

10 i _____ to sao paulo on august 24 and i started teaching there a week later.

11 i taught english in brazil _____ three years. **12** i _____ my

time there very much. **13** i will never _____ august 24, 2009. **14** that day was the

_____ of my teaching career in brazil.

ACTIVITY 14 **Guided Writing: Making Changes in Model Writing**

Write the paragraph from Activity 13 again, but make the changes listed below and all other necessary changes.

Sentence 1. Add **very** in the correct place. You will need to change another word.

Sentence 3. Change **teacher** to a different profession. Change other words about teaching in other sentences.

Sentence 4 and others. Change **Brazil** to a different country.

Sentences 4 and 5. Combine the information in these two sentences with **because.** Use the word **there** instead of the country name the second time.

Sentence 6. Change **the school** to a place that fits with the change you made in Sentence 3.

Sentence 10. Change **Sao Paulo** to a city in the country you chose in Sentence 4. Combine the clauses with **when.**

Sentences 13 and 14. Combine these two sentences with **because.**

_____

_____

_____

_____

_____

_____

_____

_____

_____

_____

_____

_____

_____

For more practice with the **grammar** in this unit, go to NGL.Cengage.com/GWF.

Building Vocabulary and Spelling

Learning Words with the Sound of u in wood*

u = w **o o** d   This sound is usually spelled with the letters **oo, u, ou,** and another spelling.

w **o o** d

p **u** s h

c **o u** l d

ACTIVITY 15 **Which Words Do You Know?**

This list has 22 common words with the sound of **u** in w**oo**d.

1. Notice the spelling patterns.

2. Check ✓ the words you know.

3. Look up new words in a dictionary. Write the meanings in your Vocabulary Notebook.

Common Words

GROUP 1:
Words spelled with **oo**

☐ **1.** b o o k

☐ **2.** c o o k

☐ **3.** c o o k i e

☐ **4.** f o o t

☐ **5.** g o o d

☐ **6.** l o o k

☐ **7.** s t o o d

☐ **8.** t o o k

☐ **9.** w o o d

☐ **10.** w o o l

☐ **11.** u n d e r s t o o d

*List is from: Spelling Vocabulary List © 2013 Keith Folse

GROUP 2:
Words spelled with **u**

☐ **12.** b **u** l l

☐ **13.** b **u** s h

☐ **14.** f **u** l l

☐ **15.** p **u** l l

☐ **16.** p **u** s h

☐ **17.** p **u** t

☐ **18.** s **u** g a r

GROUP 3:
Words spelled with **ou**

☐ **19.** c **ou** l d

☐ **20.** s h **ou** l d

☐ **21.** w **ou** l d

GROUP 4:
Other spelling

☐ **22.** w **o** m an

ACTIVITY 16 **Matching Words and Pictures**

Use the list in Activity 15 to write the common word that matches the picture.

1. _____

3. _____

2. _____

4. _____

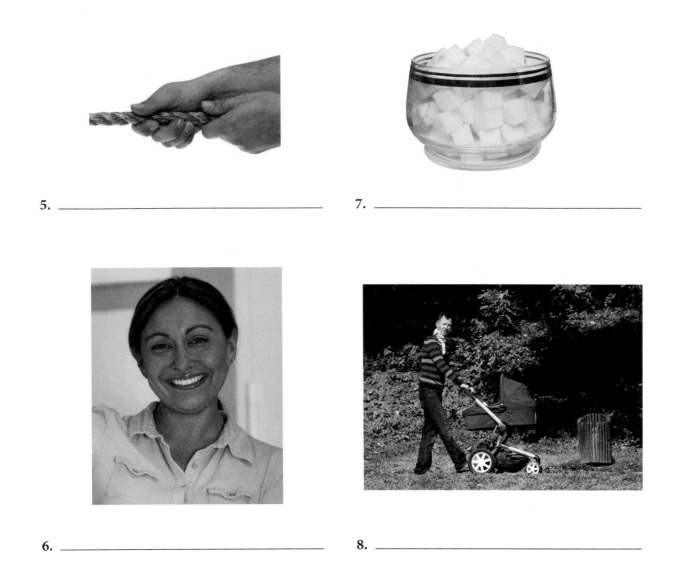

5. _____   7. _____

6. _____   8. _____

ACTIVITY 17 **Spelling Words with the Sound of <u>u</u> in w<u>oo</u>d**

Fill in the missing letters to spell words with the sound of **<u>u</u>** in w**<u>oo</u>**d. Then copy the correct word.

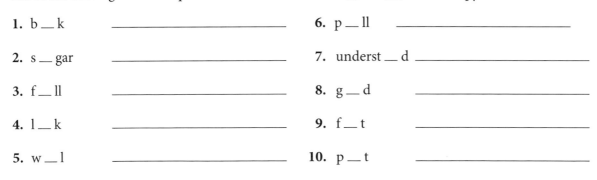

1. b __ k   _____   **6.** p __ ll   _____

2. s __ gar   _____   **7.** underst __ d _____

3. f __ ll   _____   **8.** g __ d   _____

4. l __ k   _____   **9.** f __ t   _____

5. w __ l   _____   **10.** p __ t   _____

ACTIVITY 18 **Writing Sentences with Vocabulary in Context**

Complete each sentence with the correct word from Activity 17. Then copy the sentence with correct capital letters, commas, and end punctuation.

1. the plural of .... is feet

_____

2. do you want me to .... some milk and .... in your tea

_____

3. our new boss is .... of new ideas for the company

_____

4. the .... on the table belongs to carlos

_____

5. you should never .... a plug from an outlet by its cord

_____

6. the weather is cold so it is .... for you to wear a heavy .... sweater

_____

7. maria thomas and amina .... all the words on the test yesterday so their scores were very high

_____

_____

8. zebras .... like horses with stripes

_____

ACTIVITY 19 **Scrambled Letters**

Change the order of the letters to make a word that has the sound of **u** in w**oo**d.

_____	**1.** o o k c	_____	**8.** d o w o
_____	**2.** s h u p	_____	**9.** o w m a n
_____	**3.** o u s h l d	_____	**10.** b o k o
_____	**4.** s h u b	_____	**11.** k o t o
_____	**5.** i c c o o k	_____	**12.** w u o l d
_____	**6.** t o d o s	_____	**13.** g u r s a
_____	**7.** u o c l d	_____	**14.** n d r s t d u e o o

ACTIVITY 20 **Spelling Practice**

Write the word that you hear. You will hear each word two times.

1. _____   6. _____   11. _____

2. _____   7. _____   12. _____

3. _____   8. _____   13. _____

4. _____   9. _____   14. _____

5. _____   10. _____ 15. _____

ACTIVITY 21 **Spelling Review: Which Word Is Correct?**

This review covers the different ways of spelling <u>u</u> in w<u>oo</u>d in this unit. Read each pair of words. Circle the word that is spelled correctly.

	A	B		A	B
1.	book	buk	11.	full	ful
2.	coukie	cookie	12.	should	shuld
3.	bull	boul	13.	good	gud
4.	cuod	could	14.	look	lok
5.	wuman	woman	15.	stod	stood
6.	couk	cook	16.	wod	wood
7.	pute	put	17.	boll	bull
8.	tuk	took	18.	wuld	would
9.	pul	pull	19.	sagur	sugar
10.	fut	foot	20.	wool	wol

ACTIVITY 22 **Cumulative Spelling Review**

Read the four words in each row from Units 1–12. Underline the word that is spelled correctly.

	A	B	C	D
1.	bax	box	boox	boux
2.	lenguaje	lenguaje	languaje	language
3.	meny	meany	many	mny
4.	sead	sed	sayed	said

	A	B	C	D
5.	funny	funni	funie	funy
6.	laymun	laimun	lemon	lemun
7.	estop	stob	stop	stap
8.	auful	auwful	aweful	awful
9.	plis	pliss	plese	please
10.	suger	sugar	shugar	shuger
11.	everything	evrithing	everythng	evrithng
12.	wumun	wumen	womun	women
13.	never	neaver	niver	neiver
14.	happen	hoppen	hepen	hapen
15.	could	culd	coold	cuold
16.	famos	famoso	femous	famous
17.	practike	practis	practice	proctice
18.	estudent	estuden	studen	student
19.	bicos	bicause	becos	because
20.	tuk	tok	toake	took

💻 For more practice with the **spelling and vocabulary** in this unit, go to NGL.Cengage.com/GWF.

Original Student Writing

Writing Your Ideas in Sentences or a Paragraph

Write six to twelve sentences on your own paper. Write about an important day or time in your life. (You can also write about the first time you did something, such as flew on an airplane, gave a speech in public, or got a pet.) Combine clauses with subordinating conjunctions. For help, you can follow the examples in Activity 13 (page 236) and Activity 14 (page 237). (For more information about writing a paragraph, go to Appendix 4.)

Peer Editing

Exchange papers from the above activity. Read your partner's sentences.
Then use Peer Editing Sheet 12 to make comments about the writing. Go to NGL.Cengage.com/GWF.
There is a sample in Appendix 3.

💻 For more practice with the **writing** in this unit, go to NGL.Cengage.com/GWF.

A boy gently blows bubbles at an iguana in Pevas, Peru.

OBJECTIVES **Grammar:** To learn about adverbs
Vocabulary and Spelling: To study common words with the sound of <u>ow</u> in fl<u>ow</u>er
Writing: To write about a person you know

Can you write about a person you know?

Grammar for Writing

On Monday and Tuesday, Camilla works **at a restaurant.** She is **very** tired, but she **always** does her job **carefully.**

What Is an Adverb?

✓ An **adverb** is a word that adds more information to a sentence.

sentence	I answered the difficult question.
more interesting sentence	adverb of manner adverb of degree adverb of place adverb of time I **correctly** answered the **most** difficult question in math class yesterday.

✓ An adverb can be a single word (**yesterday**) or a prepositional phrase used as an adverb (**in math class**).

✓ There are five main kinds of adverbs: **place, time, manner, frequency,** and **degree.** Each kind of adverb does a different job in a sentence.

      time   degree   frequency   place   manner
    At 5 a.m., my **very** big cat **usually** jumps **on my bed,** and I **quickly** open my eyes.

✓ **Adverbs of place** tell <u>where</u>.
   here, there, in this room

✓ **Adverbs of time** tell <u>when</u>.
   now, then, in the morning

✓ **Adverbs of manner** tell <u>how</u>.
   quickly, well, carefully

✓ **Adverbs of frequency** tell <u>how often</u>.
   always, never

✓ **Adverbs of degree** tell <u>how much</u>.
   very, so, extremely

Finding Adverbs in Sentences

Find and circle these 30 adverbs in the sentences. The number in parentheses is the number of adverbs in the sentence.

well	usually	after the news	incredibly	in our next check
so	early	in my car	carefully	between two other cars
late	loudly	at 7 a.m.	quickly	after breakfast
really	there	last month	in a hurry	to my office
never	very	extremely	at work	at our company
already	on time	at 5 a.m.	yesterday	in the meeting

More Money for Me

1. We had a very special meeting at our company yesterday, so I had to get up early. (4)

2. At 5 a.m., my alarm clock rang loudly, and I quickly opened my eyes. (3)

3. I usually take my time eating breakfast, but I ate my breakfast in a hurry. (2)

4. After breakfast, I got in my car and drove to my office. (3)

5. I arrived at work at 7 a.m. and carefully parked my car between two other cars. (4)

6. All of the other office workers were already there. (2)

7. My co-workers never arrive late, so we were able to begin the meeting on time. (3)

8. In the meeting, our boss told us some incredibly good news. (2)

9. We will receive a special bonus in our next check for working so well last month. (4)

10. After the news, everyone was extremely happy and really talkative. (3)

Adverbs of Place and Time

✓ **Adverbs of place** tell <u>where</u>.

> My new apartment is **here,** but my old apartment was **near the lake.**

✓ **Adverbs of time** tell <u>when</u>.

> Joe and I watched a movie **last night.** It ended **at 10 p.m.**

✓ The most common location for an adverb of place or time is near the end of a sentence.

>   place   time
> Queen Elizabeth II was born **in London.** She was born **in 1926.**

✓ If a sentence has both an adverb of place and an adverb of time, the adverb of place usually comes before the adverb of time. (Hint: Remember that P for <u>place</u> comes before T for <u>time</u> in the alphabet.)

>   place   time
> Queen Elizabeth II was born **in London in 1926.**

✓ An adverb of place or time can also begin a sentence, but you usually put a comma to separate it from the subject of the sentence.

✓ You do not usually use a comma after a one-word adverb such as **here** or **yesterday.**

place	**In France,** people put sugar on their popcorn.
	On the second floor of the house, there are three bedrooms and one bathroom.
	Here you can see a map of China. (no comma)
time	**In 1926,** Queen Elizabeth II was born in London.
	On January 30, 2012, Florida Bank opened a new office in downtown Miami.
	Yesterday we went to the bank and the post office. (no comma)

ACTIVITY 2   Writing Two Sentences with Adverbs of Place and Time

Change the order of the words to write two sentences. Be careful with capital letters, commas, and periods.

1. classes / my brother and sister / at 8 a.m. / begin / their

   My brother and sister begin their classes at 8 a.m.

   At 8 a.m., my brother and sister begin their classes.

2. in 2011 / were / in madrid / we

   _____

   _____

3. to the united states / jose / came / five years / martinez / ago

_____

_____

4. a pair of / at the mall / jonathan / yesterday / new / shoes / bought

_____

_____

5. are / at / going to eat / lucas / and / lunch / a steak restaurant / tomorrow / i

_____

_____

6. on / play / with maria / carla / saturday morning / i / tennis / and diana

_____

_____

Adverbs of Manner

✓ **Adverbs of manner** tell <u>how</u>.

> You should fry the meat **quickly** to keep the flavor.

✓ Most adverbs of manner consist of an adjective + **–ly**.

> adjective   adverb of manner
>
> Lim is a very **careful** driver.   Lim drives very **carefully**.

adjective	adverb	adjective	adverb
careful	carefully	quick	quickly
clear	clearly	quiet	quietly
current	currently	slow	slowly
easy	easily	sudden	suddenly

Exceptions: good ➔ **well;** fast ➔ **fast;** hard ➔ **hard**

✓ The most common location for an adverb of manner is near the end of a sentence.

> adverb
>
> Our teacher spoke **clearly.**

✓ If there is an object, the adverb goes after the object.

> object   adverb
>
> He explained all **of the new vocabulary carefully.**

ACTIVITY 3 Writing Adjectives and Adverbs of Manner in Three Sentences

Write each group of words as three complete sentences. Use the correct adjective or adverb. Be careful with capital letters, commas, and periods.

1. (quick) maria is a great student she always has a _____ answer maria answers _____

   Maria is a great student.   She always has a quick answer.
   _____

   Maria answers quickly.
   _____

2. (slow) paul is a _____ writer he likes to take his time paul writes _____

   _____

   _____

3. (good) mrs smith is a _____ teacher the students like her class a lot she explains things _____

   _____

   _____

4. (easy) i studied a lot for today's test it was an_____ test for me i answered everything _____

   _____

   _____

5. (careful) please read the questions _____ you need to understand the questions before you answer them you need to be a _____ reader

   _____

   _____

Adverbs of Frequency

✓ **Adverbs of frequency** tell <u>how often</u>.

   Kevin and I **never** eat lunch at noon. Our lunch is **always** at 11:30.

✓ Common adverbs of frequency include:

   always   usually   often   sometimes   seldom   rarely   hardly ever   never

✓ The most common location for an adverb of frequency is <u>after</u> the verb **be**, but <u>before</u> other verbs.

   I <u>am</u> **always** late to meetings.   I **always** <u>arrive</u> late to meetings.

✓ When a verb has two parts, the frequency word goes in the middle.

   I <u>can</u> **usually** <u>eat</u> a whole pizza.   People <u>should</u> **always** <u>lock</u> their doors.

✓ The word **sometimes** can occur at the beginning, middle, or end of a sentence.

beginning	**Sometimes** John and I watch TV at night.
middle	John and I **sometimes** watch TV at night.
end	John and I watch TV at night **sometimes**.

Writing Answers in Sentences with Adverbs of Frequency

Read each question and then write a sentence about yourself. Use an adverb of frequency. Use correct capital letters, commas, and periods.

1. Can you name something that you always do on Monday?
   I always wake up early on Monday.
   _____

2. What do you usually eat for breakfast?
   _____

3. Can you name something that you never eat for breakfast?
   _____

4. What is something that you seldom do in the morning?
   _____

5. What is something that your mother sometimes does on the weekend?
   _____

ACTIVITY 5 **Writing Interview Sentences Using Adverbs of Manner**

Use the five questions from Activity 4 to interview another student. On your own paper, write six sentences about that person.

Use this sentence for sentence 1: **This information is about _____.**

Then, your sentence 2 will be from question 1 in Activity 4. Your sentence 3 will be from question 2 in Activity 4, and so on.

In sentences 2 to 6, be sure to use an adverb of frequency with the information about the person you interviewed.

Use correct capital letters, commas, and periods.

Adverbs of Degree

✓ **Adverbs of degree** tell how much.

   The bus station was **very** crowded. It was **extremely** hot.

✓ Common adverbs of degree include:

   very   really   extremely   so   too   incredibly   completely

✓ The adverb of degree **too** has a negative meaning. It is not used with positive words.

   Negative meaning: The soup was **too** salty. (This use is correct.)

   Positive meaning: The soup was **too** delicious. (This use is NOT correct.)

✓ Adverbs of degree can come before an adjective or an adverb.

before an adjective	The test was **extremely** difficult.
before an adverb	She sings **really** well.

ACTIVITY 6 **Writing Adverbs of Degree in Two Sentences**

Write each pair of sentences. Use the adverb of degree in the correct place. Use correct capital letters, commas, and periods.

1. (very) i like bananas they are delicious

   I like bananas. They are very delicious.

   _____

2. (really) i like this chocolate cake a lot it is good

   _____

   _____

3. (very) the math test was difficult matt did not pass it

   _____

   _____

4. (too) jenna wants to play tennis today but it is hot maybe she will play tomorrow

   _____

   _____

5. (very) the problems in our country are serious no one can fix them

   _____

   _____

6. (extremely) everyone should vote it is an important thing to do

   _____

   _____

Common Student Mistakes

Student Mistake X	Problem	Correct Example ✓
In the early summer of **2010 my** father got a new job in London.	comma missing after adverb of time that begins a sentence	In the early summer of 2010, my father got a new job in London.
She speaks **well** English and French.	placement of adverb of manner	She speaks **English and French well**.
I do **always** my homework.	placement of adverb of frequency	I **always do** my homework.
This cheese is **too** delicious.	use of **too** with a positive word	This cheese is **really** delicious.

ACTIVITY 7 **Scrambled Sentences**

Change the order of the words to write a correct sentence. Be careful with spelling, capital letters, final punctuation, and word order. If there is a comma, it must stay with its word as shown. Do not add any commas.

The Sapporo Snow Festival

1. hokkaido is sapporo a large island is the capital in northern japan, and

   _____

2. hokkaido in the summer many japanese tourists visit because is not so hot the weather

   _____

3. because people visit see the snow and ice they want to hokkaido in the winter

   _____

4. they usually come a lot of the to sapporo snow in early february festival snow when there is

   _____

5. hokkaido has winters because it is far north, so very long

   _____

253

6. it is really cold when the weather is cold,

_____

7. is −8 °C in january, the temperature around

_____

8. buildings with the build huge snow and people animals and ice

_____

9. are beautiful these and buildings animals very

_____

10. the sapporo is one of in the world snow festival the events most famous

_____

ACTIVITY 8 **Finding and Correcting 10 Mistakes**

Circle the ten mistakes. Then write the sentences correctly. The number in parentheses ( ) is the number of mistakes in that sentence. Be ready to explain your answers.

Saudi Arabia

Studying English in Three Countries

1. Fatima is from the Saudi Arabia, and she speaks English very well. (1)

_____

2. She takes three years of English in high school, and now she takes English classes at very good university. (2)

_____

| The Netherlands | Japan |

3. Lucas and Thomas is from the Netherlands, and we speak English well. (2)

_____

4. Students in the Netherlands study English for very long time, so many of them speak English extremely well. (1)

_____

5. Kyoko is from Japan, and she is wants to improve his English conversation ability. (2)

_____

6. Students in Japan did not have many chances to use their English but many schools want to change this situation. (2)

_____

CD 2, Track 11 **ACTIVITY 9** **Dictation**

You will hear six sentences three times. Listen carefully and write the six sentences. The number in parentheses ( ) is the number of words in the sentence. Be careful with capital letters and end punctuation.

1. _____ (8)

2. _____ (6)

3. _____ (7)

4. _____ (10)

5. _____ (8)

6. _____ (12)

ACTIVITY 10 Practicing Grammar and Vocabulary in Model Writing

Read the sentences in the paragraph very carefully. Fill in the missing words from the word bank. Circle the 11 letters that need to be capital letters. Add commas in the correct places. Then copy the paragraph on your own paper.

supermarket	about	but	sometimes	from his house
every day	about	really	because	carefully

My Neighbor

1 this is a story _____ my neighbor. **2** his name is mr taylor.

3 he is _____ 80 years old but he drives his car _____.

4 he is old so he drives very _____. **5** _____ he drives very slowly many other cars pass by him. **6** he drives from his house to the _____ twice a week.

7 _____ he drives _____ to the bank. **8** mr taylor drives well _____ i am _____ afraid when i see him in his car.

Write the paragraph from Activity 10 again, but make the changes listed below and all other necessary changes.

Sentence 2. Change **Mr. Taylor** to a different name. (Look at the photo below for ideas.)

Sentence 3. Change **80** to **18**. Change **but** to **and.**

Sentence 4. Change the adjective to make it match the photo below. Make the second verb negative.

Sentence 5. Change **slowly** to its opposite. Add the word **can't** to the second verb.

Sentences 6 and 7. In these two sentences, change the places after the preposition **to.** Choose places that match the person in the photo below.

Sentence 8. Change the name to match sentence 2. Make the first verb negative. Change the word **but** to **so.**

_____

_____

_____

_____

_____

_____

_____

💻 For more practice with the **grammar** in this unit, go to NGL.Cengage.com/GWF.

Building Vocabulary and Spelling

Learning Words with the Sound of ow as in flower*

ow = f l **o w** e r   This sound is usually spelled with the letters **ou** and **ow**.

flower

house

ACTIVITY 12 **Which Words Do You Know?**

This list has 35 common words with the sound of **ow** in fl**ow**er.

1. Notice the spelling patterns.

2. Check ✓ the words you know.

3. Look up new words in a dictionary. Write the meanings in your Vocabulary Notebook.

Common Words

GROUP 1:
Words spelled with **ou**

☐ 1. a b **o u** t

☐ 2. a r **o u** n d

☐ 3. c l **o u** d

☐ 4. c **o u** n t

☐ 5. f l **o u** r

☐ 6. f **o u** n d

☐ 7. g r **o u** n d

☐ 8. h **o u** r

☐ 9. h **o u** s e

☐ 10. l **o u** d

☐ 11. m **o u** s e

☐ 12. m **o u** n t a i n

☐ 13. m **o u** t h

☐ 14. **o u** r

☐ 15. **o u** t

☐ 16. p **o u** n d

☐ 17. r **o u** n d

☐ 18. s h **o u** t

☐ 19. s **o u** n d

☐ 20. s **o u** r

☐ 21. s **o u** t h

*List is from: Spelling Vocabulary List © 2013 Keith Folse

GROUP 2:

Words spelled with **ow**

☐ 22. a l l **o w**

☐ 23. b **o w**

☐ 24. b r **o w** n

☐ 25. c **o w**

☐ 26. c r **o w** d e d

☐ 27. d **o w** n

☐ 28. f l **o w** e r

☐ 29. h **o w**

☐ 30. n **o w**

☐ 31. p **o w** e r

☐ 32. s h **o w** e r

☐ 33. t **o w** e l

☐ 34. t **o w** n

☐ 35. v **o w** e l

ACTIVITY 13 **Matching Words and Pictures**

Use the list in Activity 12 to write the common word that matches the picture.

1. _____

2. _____

3. _____

4. _____

5. _____

6. _____

7. _____

8. _____

259

ACTIVITY 14 **Spelling Words with the Sound of <u>ow</u> in fl<u>ow</u>er**

Fill in the missing letters to spell words with the sound of <u>ow</u> in fl<u>ow</u>er. Then copy the correct word.

1. t __ n   _____

2. ar __ nd   _____

3. n __   _____

4. r __ nd   _____

5. all __   _____

6. s __ nd   _____

7. s __ th   _____

8. ab __ t   _____

9. l __ d   _____

10. __ t   _____

11. c __   _____

12. h __ r   _____

ACTIVITY 15 **Writing Sentences with Vocabulary in Context**

Complete each sentence with the correct word from Activity 14. Then copy the sentence with correct capital letters, commas, and end punctuation.

1. mexico is located .... of the united states

   _____

2. when my car makes a strange .... i take it to a mechanic

   _____

3. there are sixty minutes in an ....

   _____

4. that movie is .... two people from korea

   _____

5. it is noon ....

   _____

6. i live in new york, but i was born in a small ....

   _____

7. my little brother loves to run .... the tree in our backyard

   _____

8. my parents do not .... me to drive i am too young for a license

   _____

9. a .... gives us milk

   _____

10. susan does not like that music because it is so ....

   _____

11. the opposite of in is ....

_____

12. oranges tennis balls and coins are examples of .... things

_____

ACTIVITY 16 **Scrambled Letters**

Change the order of the letters to write a word that has the sound of <u>ow</u> in fl<u>ow</u>er.

_____ **1.** r o u s

_____ **2.** e s o u h

_____ **3.** f r o w l e

_____ **4.** s n d o u

_____ **5.** o u p n d

_____ **6.** w o n d

_____ **7.** d o u l

_____ **8.** f o u r l

_____ **9.** m u s e o

_____ **10.** l o t w e

_____ **11.** o w n

_____ **12.** g o u n d r

_____ **13.** s u o h t

_____ **14.** d o f u n

CD 2, Track 12 **ACTIVITY 17** **Spelling Practice**

Write the word that you hear. You will hear each word two times.

1. _____

2. _____

3. _____

4. _____

5. _____

6. _____

7. _____

8. _____

9. _____

10. _____

11. _____

12. _____

13. _____

14. _____

15. _____

ACTIVITY 18 **Spelling Review: Which Word Is Correct?**

This review covers the different ways of spelling <u>ow</u> in fl<u>ow</u>er in this unit. Read each pair of words. Circle the word that is spelled correctly.

	A	B		A	B
1.	house	howse	11.	sour	sowr
2.	pound	pownd	12.	allou	allow
3.	our	owr	13.	found	fownd
4.	doun	down	14.	south	sowth
5.	mouth	mowth	15.	pouer	power
6.	mouse	mowse	16.	touel	towel
7.	cou	cow	17.	hou	how
8.	about	abowt	18.	shout	showt
9.	shour	shower	19.	crouded	crowded
10.	hour	howr	20.	cloud	clowd

ACTIVITY 19 **Cumulative Spelling Review**

Read the four words in each row from Units 1–13. Underline the word that is spelled correctly.

	A	B	C	D
1.	flowr	floore	flouwer	flower
2.	famows	famosu	famous	feimos
3.	kitchn	kitchin	kitchen	ketchen
4.	posible	bosibul	possible	bossible
5.	countain	counten	contain	conten
6.	shold	should	shuld	showld
7.	femli	femili	famly	family
8.	papper	pepper	peapper	pipper
9.	minits	minutes	menutes	menits
10.	studente	estudent	student	stdent

	A	B	C	D
11.	money	mony	mouney	moni
12.	haous	hows	house	hause
13.	taol	taowel	touwel	towel
14.	bcause	bcose	becose	because
15.	clothes	clotese	clouthes	clouethes
16.	finaly	finally	finali	finalli
17.	soas	saus	sauce	sose
18.	reason	renson	raisone	rason
19.	arounde	arownde	arownd	around
20.	evribody	evribady	everybady	everybody

💻 For more practice with the **spelling and vocabulary** in this unit, go to NGL.Cengage.com/GWF.

Original Student Writing

Writing Your Ideas in Sentences or a Paragraph

Write eight to twelve sentences on your own paper. Write about a person you know. This person can be a friend, neighbor, or someone famous. Be sure to use adverbs of place, time, manner, frequency, and degree. For help, you can follow the examples in Activity 10 (page 256) or Activity 11 (page 257). (For more information about writing a paragraph, go to Appendix 4.)

Peer Editing

Exchange papers from the above activity. Read your partner's sentences.
Then use Peer Editing Sheet 13 to make comments about the writing. Go to NGL.Cengage.com/GWF.
There is a sample in Appendix 3.

💻 For more practice with the **writing** in this unit, go to NGL.Cengage.com/GWF.

Verbs: Present Progressive Tense

Scientists are measuring a giant sequoia tree in Sequoia National Park, California.

OBJECTIVES **Grammar:** To learn about present progressive tense
Vocabulary and Spelling: To study common words with the sound of **oy** as in b**oy**
Writing: To write about people who are doing different things right now

Can you write about what people are doing right now?

It **is raining** now.   The sun **is not shining** now.   The man **is running** now.

Present Progressive Tense

✓ In **present progressive tense**, you use **am, is, are** with **verb + ing**.

    I **am eating**.

✓ You use present progressive tense to talk about an action that is happening now. Four common time phrases for present progressive tense are **now, right now, today,** and **this** _____.

    We **are watching** TV <u>**now**</u>.

    Michael usually drives to school, but <u>**right now**</u> he **is walking** to class.

    I **am working** hard <u>**today**</u>.

    It rained a lot last night, but the sun **is shining** <u>**this**</u> morning.

✓ To make a negative with present progressive, use **not** after **am/is/are**.

    we **are planning** → we **are** <u>**not**</u> **planning**

✓ Contractions are common in speaking, but they are not so common in formal or academic writing.

    <u>**we're**</u> **planning**   **we** <u>**aren't**</u> **planning**

✓ Verbs that do not show action are not common in present progressive tense. With non-action verbs, use simple present tense.

    Some students **need** help with their homework now. (This is correct)

    Some students <u>**are needing**</u> help with their homework now. (This is NOT correct.)

Present Progressive Tense

	work	eat	take	plan
Singular	I **am** work**ing**	I **am** eat**ing**	I **am** tak**ing**	I **am** plan**ning**
	you **are** work**ing**	you **are** eat**ing**	you **are** tak**ing**	you **are** plan**ning**
	he **is** work**ing**	he **is** eat**ing**	he **is** tak**ing**	he **is** plan**ning**
	she **is** work**ing**	she **is** eat**ing**	she **is** tak**ing**	she **is** plan**ning**
	it **is** work**ing**	it **is** eat**ing**	it **is** tak**ing**	it **is** plan**ning**
Plural	we **are** work**ing**	we **are** eat**ing**	we **are** tak**ing**	we **are** plan**ning**
	you **are** work**ing**	you **are** eat**ing**	you **are** tak**ing**	you **are** plan**ning**
	they **are** work**ing**	they **are** eat**ing**	they **are** tak**ing**	they **are** plan**ning**

✓ In present progressive tense, add **–ing** to an action verb.

    work → working   eat → eating

✓ For verbs that end in **–e**, drop the **–e** and add **–ing**.

    take → taking

✓ For verbs that end in **–ie**, change **–ie** to **–y** and add **–ing**.

    lie → lying

Single or Double Consonant?

One Syllable	
+ –ing	double consonant + –ing
clean**ing**	plan**ning**
wash**ing**	stop**ping**

Two Syllables	
+ –ing	double consonant + –ing
open**ing**	occur**ring**
happen**ing**	permit**ting**

✓ For one-syllable verbs that end in consonant + vowel + consonant (CVC), double the last letter before adding **–ing.**

    plan → planning

✓ For two-syllable verbs that end in consonant + vowel + consonant (CVC), double the last letter before adding **–ing** if the pronunciation stress is on the second syllable.

    o pen → opening   be gin → beginning

ACTIVITY 1 **Identifying Verbs in Present Progressive Tense**

Read this information about a man on an airplane. Underline the eight examples of present progressive tense. Then write them on the correct lines.

> Jacob is a passenger on Flight 873. He is flying to California. He is going there because his company is doing business there. Right now Jacob is not talking to anyone. He is not eating anything. He is not drinking anything. Jacob is working on his computer. He is listening to his favorite music. He is a very happy person right now.

subject + am / is / are (not) + verb + ing

1. _____ _____ _____

2. _____ _____ _____

3. _____ _____ _____

4. _____ _____ _____

subject + am / is / are (not) + verb + ing

5. _____ _____ _____

6. _____ _____ _____

7. _____ _____ _____

8. _____ _____ _____

Write the **–ing** form of the 30 most common verbs in English writing.

verb	–ing form		verb	–ing form
1. go	_____		16. watch	_____
2. try	_____		17. give	_____
3. look	_____		18. sit	_____
4. make	_____		19. wait	_____
5. get	_____		20. live	_____
6. use	_____		21. see	_____
7. say	_____		22. leave	_____
8. come	_____		23. stand	_____
9. work	_____		24. hold	_____
10. talk	_____		25. tell	_____
11. take	_____		26. ask	_____
12. run	_____		27. think	_____
13. play	_____		28. move	_____
14. decide	_____		29. put	_____
15. try	_____		30. follow	_____

Source: Corpus of Contemporary American English

Use one word from each of the three groups to make five new sentences. Be careful with capital letters, verb form (**–ing**), and periods.

Subject	Action	Time
she	live in Canada	now
I	try to find a new job	right now
they	sit on a bench	at this moment

1. _____

2. _____

3. _____

4. _____

5. _____

ACTIVITY 4 **PAIR WORK: Who Has the Most Sentences that Are Different?**

Work with another student. Compare your sentences from Activity 3. You receive one point for each sentence that your partner does not have.

    1st time: _____ / 5 points possible

When you finish, work with another student. Each different sentence receives one point.

    2nd time: _____ / 5 points possible

    Your total: _____ / 10 points possible

Common Student Mistakes

Student Mistake X	Problem	Correct Example ✓
Jessica **is eating** lunch at 12:30 every day.	wrong tense	Jessica **eats** lunch at 12:30 every day.
Jessica **eats** lunch right now.	wrong tense	Jessica **is eating** lunch right now.
Now **we planning** our vacation.	form of **be** missing	Now we **are** planning our vacation.
Ali and I are **cook** spaghetti now.	**–ing** verb ending missing	Ali and I are cook**ing** spaghetti now.
I am **writeing** an e-mail now.	verb not spelled correctly	I am **writing** an e-mail now.
Some students **are needing** help with their homework now.	present progressive with non-action verb	Some students **need** help with their homework now.

ACTIVITY 5 **Correcting Mistakes with Present Progressive Verbs in Context**

Each sentence has a mistake with a verb. Correct this mistake and write the sentence again. Pay attention to capital letters and periods.

A Family Vacation

1. the johnson family taking a trip today

_____

2. they are go to california

_____

3. mr. johnson is driveing

_____

4. the children listen to the radio

_____

5. they are enjoy this trip very much

_____

ACTIVITY 6 Scrambled Sentences

Change the order of the words to write a correct sentence. Be careful with spelling, capital letters, punctuation, and word order.

At the Supermarket

1. at the supermarket now lucas is shopping right

_____

2. many things he buying is

_____

3. dinner for cousin's planning a lucas is his big birthday

_____

4. delicious dinner for tonight's getting some big food he is

_____

5. right waiting in now is lucas line

_____

6. but the hard little cashier she is a is working very slow

_____

7. lucas is watch his he is thinking about the because looking at time

_____

8. great cousin to his a have lucas wants dinner with

_____

Circle the ten mistakes. Then write the sentences correctly. The number in parentheses ( ) is the number of mistakes in that sentence. Be ready to explain your answers.

A Day at the Zoo

1. Much people are visit the zoo today. (2)

   _____

2. Two giraffes eating leaf from the tall trees. (2)

   _____

3. An elephant is drink some water. (1)

   _____

4. Right now some children are laugh at the monkeys funny. (2)

   _____

5. One child pointing to the sky because an airplane is fly overhead. (2)

   _____

6. Everyone has a good time at the zoo today. (1)

   _____

 **ACTIVITY 8** Dictation

You will hear six sentences three times. Listen carefully and write the six sentences. The number in parentheses ( ) is the number of words. Be careful with capital letters and end punctuation.

1. _____ (13)

2. _____ (10)

3. _____ (13)

4. _____ (9)

5. _____ (6)

6. _____ (9)

ACTIVITY 9 **Practicing Grammar and Vocabulary in Model Writing**

Read the sentences in the paragraph very carefully. Fill in the missing words from the word bank. Circle the 23 letters that need to be capital letters. Add periods and commas in the correct places. Then copy the paragraph on your own paper.

son	care	put	so	because
not	last	floor	on	difficult
has	dead	made	in	folded

Time to Clean the Hill Family's House

1 mr and mrs hill and their four children live in a very big house _____ maple street _____ chicago. **2** their house _____ five bedrooms two bathrooms a kitchen a dining room a huge living room and a garage. **3** they cleaned their house _____ saturday. **4** mr hill took _____ of the yard. **5** he picked up all the _____ leaves and he put them in trash bags. **6** mrs. hill washed all the dishes, and she _____ them in the cupboard. **7** sarah mopped the kitchen _____ and anna _____ all the beds. **8** their youngest daughter _____ towels. **9** their _____ cleaned one of the bathrooms. **10** he did _____ like this job. **11** it was _____ to clean this big house _____ everyone helped. **12** _____ everyone did their jobs so well the hill family's house was beautiful.

ACTIVITY 10 **Guided Writing: Making Changes in Model Writing**

Write the sentences from Activity 9 again, but your new sentences are about right now. Make the changes listed below and all other necessary changes.

<u>Sentence 3</u>. Change **last Saturday** to **today**. Then change the verb tense of all the action verbs.

<u>Sentences 9 and 10</u>. Combine these two sentences with a good connecting word. Use the simple present tense for the verb **like**.

<u>Sentence 12</u>. Write a new sentence that talks about their house all the time. In other words, the sentence should be a fact, not only a statement about right now.

_____

_____

_____

_____

_____

_____

_____

_____

_____

_____

_____

For more practice with the **grammar** in this unit, go to NGL.Cengage.com/GWF.

Building Vocabulary and Spelling

Learning Words with the Sound of oy as in boy*

oy = b oy   This sound is usually spelled with the letters **oy** and **oi.**

b o y

c o i n

ACTIVITY 11 **Which Words Do You Know?**

This list has 16 words with the sound of **oy** in b**oy**.

1. Notice the spelling patterns.

2. Check ✓ the words you know.

3. Look up new words in a dictionary. Write the meanings in your Vocabulary Notebook.

Common Words

GROUP 1:
Words spelled with **oy**

- ☐ **1.** b o y
- ☐ **2.** d e s t r o y
- ☐ **3.** e m p l o y e e
- ☐ **4.** e m p l o y e r
- ☐ **5.** e n j o y
- ☐ **6.** j o y
- ☐ **7.** t o y

GROUP 2:
Words spelled with **oi**

- ☐ **8.** b o i l
- ☐ **9.** c h o i c e
- ☐ **10.** c o i n
- ☐ **11.** j o i n
- ☐ **12.** n o i s e
- ☐ **13.** o i l
- ☐ **14.** p o i n t
- ☐ **15.** p o i s o n
- ☐ **16.** v o i c e

*List is from: Spelling Vocabulary List © 2013 Keith Folse

ACTIVITY 12 Matching Words and Pictures

Use the list in Activity 11 to write the common word that matches the picture.

1. _____

2. _____

3. _____

4. _____

5. _____

6. _____

7. _____

8. _____

Spelling Words with the Sound of <u>oy</u> in b<u>oy</u>

Fill in the missing letters to spell words with the sound of <u>oy</u> in b<u>oy</u>. Then copy the correct word.

1. enj __   _____

2. p __ nt   _____

3. empl __ er   _____

4. destr __   _____

5. ch __ ce   _____

6. v __ ce   _____

7. b __ l   _____

8. c __ n   _____

ACTIVITY 14   **Writing Sentences with Vocabulary in Context**

Complete each sentence with the correct word from Activity 13. Then copy the sentence with correct capital letters, commas, and end punctuation.

1. an orange a tennis ball and a .... are examples of round things

    _____

2. who is your ....

    _____

3. a strong storm can .... houses and buildings

    _____

4. it takes about four or five minutes to .... an egg

    _____

5. the three arrows .... to the location of the cash machine

    _____

6. for the main course of your dinner you have a .... of chicken fish or beef

    _____

7. most people do not .... movies with sad endings

    _____

8. people want to listen to her songs because she has an incredible ....

    _____

ACTIVITY 15 Scrambled Letters

Change the order of the letters to write a word that has the sound of **oy** in b**oy**.

_____ 1. c h c e o i

_____ 2. e c o i v

_____ 3. j y o

_____ 4. l o i

_____ 5. e e e o m p l y

_____ 6. e s i o n

_____ 7. b i o l

_____ 8. n i o j

_____ 9. y o b

_____ 10. d e t r s o y

_____ 11. j y o e n

_____ 12. s o p i o n

_____ 13. y o t

_____ 14. t o i n p

CD 2,
Track 14 ACTIVITY 16 Spelling Practice

Write the word that you hear. You will hear each word two times.

1. _____

2. _____

3. _____

4. _____

5. _____

6. _____

7. _____

8. _____

9. _____

10. _____

11. _____

12. _____

13. _____

14. _____

15. _____

ACTIVITY 17 Spelling Review: Which Word Is Correct?

This review covers the different ways of spelling **oy** in b**oy** in this unit. Read each pair of words. Circle the word that is spelled correctly.

	A	B		A	B
1.	boyl	boil	9.	choyce	choice
2.	boy	boi	10.	voyce	voice
3.	oyl	oil	11.	joy	joi
4.	destroy	destroi	12.	enjoy	enjoi
5.	poyson	poison	13.	coyn	coin
6.	poynt	point	14.	noyse	noise
7.	employee	emploiee	15.	employer	emploier
8.	joyn	join			

Read the four words in each row from Units 1–14. Underline the word that is spelled correctly.

	A	B	C	D
1.	shoice	choice	choise	echoise
2.	nex	naxt	next	nax
3.	gools	goals	gouls	goels
4.	suger	asugar	esugar	sugar
5.	bcause	bcose	becose	because
6.	reason	reeson	raison	rason
7.	with	weth	whit	whith
8.	piple	beeble	people	peepl
9.	tomorrow	tomorow	tamorrow	temorow
10.	famil	familia	famili	family
11.	dstroy	destroie	distroy	destroy
12.	spind	spnd	spend	espend
13.	enclude	include	includ	enclud
14.	shwer	eshower	showr	shower
15.	doctere	doctor	dokter	ductor
16.	righ	rait	right	raight
17.	noyse	niose	noise	nois
18.	allways	alwes	allwes	always
19.	doughter	duter	doter	daughter
20.	hungry	hungrey	hungri	humgrey

For more practice with the **spelling and vocabulary** in this unit, go to NGL.Cengage.com/GWF.

Original Student Writing

Writing Your Ideas in Sentences or a Paragraph

Write eight to twelve sentences on your own paper. Write about people who are doing different things right now. For example, write about some people in a restaurant, in school, in a park, or another place. Use the present progressive tense. For help, you can follow the examples in Activity 9 (page 274) and Activity 10 (page 275). (For more information about writing a paragraph, go to Appendix 4.)

Peer Editing

Exchange papers from the above activity. Read your partner's sentences.
Then use Peer Editing Sheet 14 to make comments about the writing. Go to NGL.Cengage.com/GWF. There is a sample in Appendix 3.

For more practice with the **writing** in this unit, go to NGL.Cengage.com/GWF.

Brief Writer's Handbook

Appendices

Writing the English Alphabet

A a	B b	C c	D d	E e	F f	G g	H h	I i	J j
K k	L l	M m	N n	O o	P p	Q q	R r	S s	T t
U u	V v	W w	X x	Y y	Z z				

✓ There are 26 letters in the English alphabet.

    5 are vowels: A E I O U

    21 are consonants: B C D F G H J K L M N P Q R S T V W X Y Z

✓ When **w** and **y** come after a vowel, these two letters are silent vowels: **saw, grow, play, toy, buy.**

✓ When **w** and **y** are at the beginning of a syllable, they are consonant sounds: **wake, wish, when, year, young.**

Using Capitalization in Your Writing

Rule	Example
1. the first word in a sentence	**T**he weather today is good.
2. the pronoun **I**	Maria and **I** live in New York.
3. people's formal and professional titles	**D**r. Johnson works with **M**rs. Smith.
4. proper names (specific people and places)	My brother and **T**im visited **F**ifth **A**venue in **N**ew **Y**ork.
5. languages and nationalities	Many **S**wiss can speak **G**erman, **F**rench, and **I**talian.
6. the first word and important words in titles (Prepositions, conjunctions, and articles are not important words in a title.)	*The **S**ocial **N**etwork* *Beauty and the **B**east*

    Do not use capital letters in the middle of a word: AraBic → **Arabic**

    Do not use all capital letters: JOE IS FROM BRAZIL. → **Joe is from Brazil.**

Punctuation for Writing: Periods, Question Marks, and Commas

Rule	Example
1. Put a period at the end of a statement.	The weather today is good**.**
2. Put a question mark at the end of a question.	What is the capital of South Korea**?**
3. Put a period after an abbreviation.	The **U.S.** flag has fifty stars and thirteen stripes.
4. Put a comma after each item in a list of three or more.	My favorite colors are **blue, green, and red.**
5. Do not put a comma when the list has only two items.	My favorite colors are **blue and red.**

6. Put a comma after **and, but, so,** and **or** when they connect two sentences (independent clauses).	My job is sometimes difficult**, but** I like it a lot.
7. Put a comma after the first clause when a sentence begins with **after, before, because, when,** and **if.**	**After I finished** the test**,** I called my sister.
8. Do not use a comma with **after, before, because, when,** and **if** in the second part of a sentence.	I called my sister **after I finished the test.**
9. Use a comma after a short phrase at the beginning of a sentence.	**At the end of the story,** the man and woman get married.

Parts of Speech for Writing

Part of Speech	Definition	Example
noun	the name of a person, place, or thing	**Mr. Miller, the store, car**
verb	a word that shows action or existence	**eat, is**
pronoun	a word that can take the place of a noun	**she, they**
adjective	a word that describes a noun or pronoun	**smart**
adverb	a word that talks about a verb, an adjective, or another adverb	She types **quickly.** She is **very** smart. She writes **very well.**
conjunction	a word that connects words, phrases, or sentences	red **and** green in books **or** in magazines It rained **before** the game began. The movie is long, **but** it is good.
preposition	a word that shows the relationship between a noun or pronoun and the rest of the sentence	The book **about** flying kites is **in** the bag **on** the table.
interjection	a word that shows strong emotion or excitement	**Wow! Great!**

Useful Verb Tenses for Writing

Verb Tense	Affirmative	Negative	Usage
Simple Present	I **work** you **take** he **studies** she **does** we **play** they **have**	I **do not work** you **do not take** he **does not study** she **does not do** we **do not play** they **do not have**	• for routines, habits, and other actions that happen regularly • for facts and general truths
Simple Past	I **worked** you **took** he **studied** she **did** we **played** they **had**	I **did not work** you **did not take** he **did not study** she **did not do** we **did not play** they **did not have**	• for actions that are finished

Present Progressive	I **am working**	I **am not working**	• for actions that are happening now
	you **are taking**	you **are not taking**	• for future actions if a future time adverb is used or understood
	he **is studying**	he **is not studying**	
	she **is doing**	she **is not doing**	
	we **are playing**	we **are not playing**	
	they **are having***	they **are not having***	
Future *(be going to)*	I **am going to work**	I **am not going to work**	• for future actions
	you **are going to take**	you **are not going to take**	
	he **is going to study**	he **is not going to study**	
	she **is going to do**	she **is not going to do**	
	we **are going to play**	we **are not going to play**	
	they **are going to have**	they **are not going to have**	
Future *(will)*	I **will work**	I **will not work**	• for future actions
	you **will take**	you **will not take**	
	he **will study**	he **will not study**	
	she **will do**	she **will not do**	
	we **will play**	we **will not play**	
	they **will have**	they **will not have**	
Present Perfect	I **have worked**	I **have not worked**	• for actions that began in the past and continue until the present
	you **have taken**	you **have not taken**	• for actions in the indefinite past time
	he **has studied**	he **has not studied**	
	she **has done**	she **has not done**	• for repeated actions in the past
	we **have played**	we **have not played**	
	they **have had**	they **have not had**	
Past Progressive	I **was working**	I **was not working**	• for longer actions that are interrupted by other actions or events
	you **were taking**	you **were not taking**	
	he **was studying**	he **was not studying**	
	she **was doing**	she **was not doing**	
	we **were playing**	we **were not playing**	
	they **were having***	they **were not having***	

* **Have** can be used in progressive tenses only when it has an active meaning in special expressions, such as

- **have** a party
- **have** a good time
- **have** a bad time
- **have** a baby

To show time relationship	after	**After** we ate dinner, we went to a movie.
	before	We ate dinner **before** we went to a movie.
	until	I will not call you **until** I finish studying.
	while	**While** the pasta is cooking, I will cut the vegetables.
	as	**As** I was leaving the office, it started to rain.
To show condition	if	**If** it rains tomorrow, we will stay home.
	even if	We will go to the park **even if** it rains tomorrow.

Appendix 1

Keeping a Vocabulary Notebook

Vocabulary is very important in speaking, listening, reading, and writing, so you need to improve your vocabulary in English. There are many words you do not know yet. The best way for you to really improve your vocabulary is to do more than study from your teacher or this book. You also need to keep a vocabulary notebook.

A vocabulary notebook is a notebook in which you write down all the new words and phrases that you do not know but you think are important. When you find a new word, write it in your notebook. However, writing words in the notebook is not enough. You also need to review the words many times.

The most important thing about learning foreign language vocabulary is the number of times you think about the word, listen to it, read it, speak it, or write it. That is your goal: to practice each word several times. You can practice any way you want.

There are many ways to organize a vocabulary notebook, and you should choose a way that you like. It is important to remember this is your notebook, and it should be useful for you. Here is one way to keep a vocabulary notebook. You write four pieces of information about each new word, but you can write as little or as much as you want.

1. Write the English word first.

2. Write a translation in your first language.

3. Write a simple definition or synonym in English.

4. Write a phrase or sentence with the word. Use a blank _____ instead of writing the word.

With these four kinds of information, you can practice the new vocabulary four ways.

Leave a lot of white space between the words and the information you write. Each page of your notebook should have only five to eight words. The white space makes the notebook neat, and you are more likely to open a clean notebook and study from it than a messy one. In addition, as you learn new information about the word, you can write that information right there in the white space. For example, if you learn that **dozen** is also used with roses, you can add **one** _____ **flowers** to the list.

Here are two examples:

From a Spanish speaker:

17. dozen   12 things

     docena   a ---------- eggs

From an Arabic speaker:

18. hot   not cold

    حار   The sun is very ----------.

Good luck with your vocabulary notebook!

Appendix 2

Additional Topics for Writing

The best way to improve your writing is to write every day. Do one of these writing practices every day. This work is in addition to the work you do for your class.

Unit 1

Writing Practice 1	Write ten sentences about ten different animals.
Writing Practice 2	Write ten sentences about different kinds of fruit or vegetables.
Writing Practice 3	Pretend that you are a famous man. Introduce yourself with "My name is …." Write ten sentences about yourself, your family, and your friends.
Writing Practice 4	Pretend that you are a famous woman. Introduce yourself with "My name is …." Write ten sentences about yourself, your family, and your friends.
Writing Practice 5	Write ten sentences about ten different cities.
Writing Practice 6	Write ten sentences with any ten of these words: **animal, apple, aunt, banana, bank, class, family, flag, January, language, man, map, math, salad, taxi.** Underline these words in your sentences.
Writing Practice 7	Write ten sentences with any ten of these words: **after, answer, ask, at, bad, can, happen, happy, has, have, last, laugh, sad, travel, understand.** Underline these words in your sentences.
Writing Practice 8	Write five sentences using one word from Practice 6 and one word from Practice 7 in each sentence. Underline these words in your sentences.
Writing Practice 9	Write ten sentences with ten new words from this book or your dictionary. Underline the new words in your sentences.
Writing Practice 10	Write ten sentences about yourself.

Unit 2

Writing Practice 11	Write ten sentences with these words: **Paris, Arabic, January, California, Anna, Pepsi, Toyota, Saudi Arabia, Mexico, Saturday.** Underline these words in your sentences.
Writing Practice 12	Write ten sentences about ten of your classmates, friends, or family members.
Writing Practice 13	Pretend that you are a girl from China. Introduce yourself with "My name is …." Write ten sentences about yourself, your family, and your friends.
Writing Practice 14	Pretend that you are a boy from Brazil. Introduce yourself with "My name is …." Write ten sentences about yourself, your family, and your friends.
Writing Practice 15	Write ten sentences about ten different countries.
Writing Practice 16	Write ten sentences with any ten of these words: **bed, bread, breakfast, egg, exercise, friend, leg, men, pen, pet, seven, test, weather, yellow.** Underline these words in your sentences.
Writing Practice 17	Write ten sentences with any ten of these words: **again, already, best, dead, enter, every, help, many, never, next, ready, said, tell, when.** Underline these words in your sentences.
Writing Practice 18	Write five sentences using one word from Practice 16 and one word from Practice 17 in each sentence. Underline these words in your sentences.
Writing Practice 19	Write ten sentences with ten new words from this book or your dictionary. Underline the new words in your sentences.
Writing Practice 20	Write ten sentences about ten people you know.

Unit 3

Writing Practice 21	Write ten sentences about what you do on different days of the week.
Writing Practice 22	Pretend you are a teacher. Write ten sentences about what you do on different days of the week.
Writing Practice 23	Write ten sentences about what your teacher does on different days of the week.
Writing Practice 24	Write three sentences with **have** and three sentences with **has**. Write two negative sentences with **do not have** and two with **does not have**.
Writing Practice 25	Write five true negative sentences about yourself. Write five true negative sentences about another person.
Writing Practice 26	Write ten sentences with any ten of these words: **bridge, chicken, city, dinner, kitchen, minute, sister, sing, six, spring, swim, will, winter, women.** Underline these words in your sentences.
Writing Practice 27	Write ten sentences with any ten of these words: **big, busy, delicious, difficult, different, give, it, list, live, milk, sit, pretty, six, this, which, with.** Underline these words in your sentences.
Writing Practice 28	Write five sentences with one word from Practice 26 and one word from Practice 27 in each sentence. Underline these words in your sentences.

Writing Practice 29	Write ten sentences with any ten of the verbs in *20 Verbs You Need to Know* (page 36). Use at least five negative verbs. Underline these words in your sentences.
Writing Practice 30	Write ten sentences about people you know. Tell what they do in real life. Do not use the verb **be**.

Unit 4

Writing Practice 31	Write ten sentences with a descriptive adjective after **is** or **are**. (An elephant is <u>big</u>.)
Writing Practice 33	Write ten sentences with a descriptive adjective before a noun. (I see a <u>big</u> elephant.)
Writing Practice 33	Write ten sentences about ten places. Use a descriptive adjective in each sentence.
Writing Practice 34	Write ten sentences that are simple definitions with **a/an** + descriptive adjective + noun. (A cat is <u>a good pet</u>. Seven is <u>an odd number</u>.)
Writing Practice 35	Write ten sentences about a person, a place, or a thing. Use a descriptive adjective in each sentence.
Writing Practice 36	Write ten sentences with any ten of these words: **body, bother, box, cotton, comma, everybody, father, hot, impossible, lock, not, rob, shop, stop.** Underline these words in your sentences.
Writing Practice 37	Write ten sentences with any ten of these words: **clock, common, doctor, drop, God, hot, job, lot, October, possible, pot, rock, socks, somebody, top.** Underline these words in your sentences.
Writing Practice 38	Write five sentences with one word from Practice 36 and one word from Practice 37 in each sentence. Underline these words in your sentences.
Writing Practice 39	Write ten sentences with at least ten of the adjectives in *20 Descriptive Adjectives You Need to Know* (page 59). Underline these adjectives in your sentences. Use at least five negative verbs.
Writing Practice 40	Write five sentences with two descriptive adjectives in each sentence. (I have a <u>red</u> shirt and <u>black</u> shoes.)

Unit 5

Writing Practice 41	Write ten sentences about people and their jobs. (My uncle is a taxi driver.)
Writing Practice 42	Write ten sentences with descriptive adjectives. Use **is** in five sentences and **are** in five sentences.
Writing Practice 43	Write five sentences with **is not** and five sentences with **are not.**
Writing Practice 44	Write ten sentences about a city and its country. (London is in England.)
Writing Practice 45	Write ten negative sentences about a city and an incorrect country. (London is not in Turkey.)
Writing Practice 46	Write ten sentences with any ten of these words: **bus, brother, company, continue, cup, cut, just, money, month, mother, must, number, run, Sunday, under.** Underline these words in your sentences.
Writing Practice 47	Write ten sentences with any ten of these words: **above, action, another, come, country, cousin, famous, funny, lunch, none, question, summer, young.** Underline these words in your sentences.
Writing Practice 48	Write five sentences with one word from Practice 46 and one word from Practice 47 in each sentence. Underline these words in your sentences.
Writing Practice 49	Write ten sentences about two businesses or companies.
Writing Practice 50	Write ten sentences about two restaurants.

Unit 6

Writing Practice 51	Write ten sentences about birds, cats, or snakes.
Writing Practice 52	Write ten sentences about a famous person. Use subject and object pronouns.
Writing Practice 53	Write two sentences with each of these pronouns: **I, me, he, him, she, her, we, us, they, them.**
Writing Practice 54	Write ten sentences with a preposition (**about, for, of, to, with, without**) and **me, you, him, her, us, them.** (This book is <u>for us</u>.)
Writing Practice 55	Think of a gift you can buy for your friend. Write ten negative sentences about your gift. (It is not very big.)
Writing Practice 56	Write ten sentences with any ten of these words: **age, break, change, day, game, grade, late, main, page, play, state, steak, take, today, wait.** Underline these words in your sentences.
Writing Practice 57	Write ten sentences with any ten of these words: **afraid, face, great, holiday, make, maybe, neighbor, paper, place, pray, rain, say, they, train, wake.** Underline these words in your sentences.
Writing Practice 58	Write five sentences with one word from Practice 56 and one word from Practice 57 in each sentence. Underline these words in your sentences.
Writing Practice 59	Write about ten people and their hobbies. Use subject and object pronouns.
Writing Practice 60	Write about two people and their families. Use subject and object pronouns.

Unit 7

Writing Practice 61	Write ten sentences with two subjects connected with **and** in each sentence. (<u>My brother</u> **and** <u>my sister</u> are tall.)
Writing Practice 62	Write ten sentences with two objects connected with **and** in each sentence. (I like <u>coffee</u> **and** <u>tea</u>.)
Writing Practice 63	Write ten sentences about any two animals. (A horse and a camel can run.)
Writing Practice 64	Write ten sentences with three words connected with **and** in each sentence. (My favorite colors are green, blue, and red.)
Writing Practice 65	Write ten sentences about things you do on two or three days. (I play tennis on Saturday and Sunday.)
Writing Practice 66	Write ten sentences with any ten of these words: **between, cheap, clean, country, dream, eat, leave, money, near, only, people, receive, sleep, story, teeth.** Underline these words in your sentences.
Writing Practice 67	Write ten sentences with any ten of these words: **beans, believe, cheese, city, easy, every, necessary, need, speak, street, teach, team, tree, week, year.** Underline these words in your sentences.

Writing Practice 68	Write five sentences with one word from Practice 66 and one word from Practice 67 in each sentence. Underline these words in your sentences.
Writing Practice 69	Write ten sentences that give two examples of one thing. (Two examples of countries are Canada and Saudi Arabia.)
Writing Practice 70	Write ten sentences with two adjectives connected with **and** in each sentence. (The parrot is colorful and loud.)

Unit 8

Writing Practice 71	Write ten sentences with **a**.
Writing Practice 72	Write ten sentences with **an**.
Writing Practice 73	Write ten sentences with **the**.
Writing Practice 74	Write ten sentences about what people in different jobs use at work. (A teacher uses a book at work.)
Writing Practice 75	Write ten sentences about what people in different jobs do not use at work. (A teacher does not use a radio at work.)
Writing Practice 76	Write ten sentences with any ten of these words: **by, decide, die, eyes, find, idea, inside, kind, light, rice, ride, sky, time, wife, write.** Underline these words in your sentences.
Writing Practice 77	Write ten sentences with any ten of these words: **arrive, behind, buy, drive, flight, high, knife, life, night, price, quiet, right, size, tie, try.** Underline these words in your sentences.
Writing Practice 78	Write five sentences with one word from Practice 76 and one word from Practice 77 in each sentence. Underline these words in your sentences.
Writing Practice 79	Write ten sentences about how to cook something.
Writing Practice 80	Write ten sentences about how to do something. Examples: how to study, how to swim, how to wash your clothes.

Unit 9

Writing Practice 81	Write ten sentences with a prepositional phrase.
Writing Practice 82	Write ten sentences about the location of items in a grocery store. Use a prepositional phrase in each sentence.
Writing Practice 83	Write ten sentences with **at** + a time.
Writing Practice 84	Write ten sentences with **on** + a day.
Writing Practice 85	Write ten sentences with **in** + a month, a season, or a year.
Writing Practice 86	Write ten sentences with any ten of these words: **alone, below, clothes, cold, follow, goal, grow, home, know, November, ocean, open, smoke, soap, window.** Underline these words in your sentences.
Writing Practice 87	Write ten sentences with any ten of these words: **also, both, close, coat, gold, goes, hope, joke, low, most, nobody, only, show, stove, yellow.** Underline these words in your sentences.
Writing Practice 88	Write five sentences with one word from Practice 86 and one word from Practice 87 in each sentence. Underline these words in your sentence.
Writing Practice 89	Write ten sentences with at least ten of the prepositions in *20 Prepositions You Need to Know* (page 159). Underline these prepositions in your sentences. Use at least five negative verbs.
Writing Practice 90	Write ten sentences with the preposition combinations on page 167. Underline these preposition combinations in your sentences.

Unit 10

Writing Practice 91	Write ten sentences with two clauses connected with **and.**
Writing Practice 92	Write ten sentences with two clauses connected with **but.**
Writing Practice 93	Write ten sentences with two clauses connected with **so** when it means "therefore."
Writing Practice 94	Write ten sentences with two clauses connected with **so** when it means "in order to."
Writing Practice 95	Write ten sentences about a person. Use two clauses with **and, but,** or **so** in at least five of your sentences.
Writing Practice 96	Write ten sentences with any ten of these words: **blue, choose, confused, do, fruit, group, include, news, pool, school, soup, tooth, you, who.** Underline these words in your sentences.
Writing Practice 97	Write ten sentences with any ten of these words: **computer, a few, food, juice, music, noon, new, shoe, soon, spoon, too, true, Tuesday, use, zoo.** Underline these words in your sentences.
Writing Practice 98	Write five sentences with one word from Practice 96 and one word from Practice 97 in each sentence. Underline these words in your sentences.
Writing Practice 99	Write five compound sentences about the job of a pilot.
Writing Practice 100	Write five compound sentences about the oldest person that you know.

Unit 11

Writing Practice 101	Write ten sentences with the past tense of at least ten of the *29 Most Common Regular Past Tense Verbs in Writing* in Activity 1 (page 205). Underline these verbs in your sentences.
Writing Practice 102	Write ten negative sentences with the past tense of at least ten of the *29 Most Common Regular Past Tense Verbs in Writing* in Activity 1 (page 205). Underline these verbs in your sentences.
Writing Practice 103	Write ten sentences with the past tense of at least ten of the *30 Most Common Irregular Past Tense Verbs in Writing* in Activity 4 (page 207). Underline these verbs in your sentences.
Writing Practice 104	Write ten negative sentences with past tense of at least ten of the *30 Most Common Irregular Past Tense Verbs in Writing* in Activity 4 (page 207). Underline these verbs in your sentences.
Writing Practice 105	Write ten sentences about what you did yesterday.

Writing Practice 106	Write ten sentences with any ten of these words: **all, almost, author, awful, bought, cough, daughter, long, raw, salt, small, song, thought, wall.** Underline these words in your sentences.
Writing Practice 107	Write ten sentences with any ten of these words: **also, always, brought, cause, draw, fall, law, sauce, saw, strong, straw, tall, talk, walk, wrong.** Underline these words in your sentences.
Writing Practice 108	Write five sentences with one word from Practice 106 and one word from Practice 107 in each sentence. Underline these words in your sentences.
Writing Practice 109	Write five compound sentences about what you did last week.
Writing Practice 110	Write ten sentences about a very important day in someone else's life.

Unit 12

Writing Practice 111	Write ten sentences with **because.** Write five with simple present tense. Write five with simple past tense.
Writing Practice 112	Write ten sentences with **before.** Write five with simple present tense. Write five with simple past tense.
Writing Practice 113	Write ten sentences with **after.** Write five with simple present tense. Write five with simple past tense.
Writing Practice 114	Write ten sentences with **when.** Write five affirmative sentences and five negative sentences.
Writing Practice 115	Write ten sentences with **if.** Write five that begin with an **if**-clause. Write five that end with an **if**-clause.
Writing Practice 116	Write eight sentences with any eight of these words: **bush, cook, could, full, good, pull, should, stood, wool, understood, woman.** Underline these words in your sentences.
Writing Practice 117	Write eight sentences with any eight of these words: **book, bull, cookie, foot, look, push, put, sugar, took, wood, would.** Underline these words in your sentences.
Writing Practice 118	Write five sentences with one word from Practice 116 and one word from Practice 117 in each sentence. Underline these words in your sentences.
Writing Practice 119	Write ten sentences with dependent clauses with **after, because, before, if, when** to tell a children's story that you know.
Writing Practice 120	Write ten sentences about something in the news yesterday. Use dependent clauses with **after, because, before, if, when** in at least five of your sentences.

Unit 13

Writing Practice 121	Write ten sentences using adverbs of place to tell where something happens or happened.
Writing Practice 122	Write ten sentences using adverbs of time to tell when something happens or happened.
Writing Practice 123	Write ten sentences using adverbs of manner to tell how something happens or happened.
Writing Practice 124	Write ten sentences using adverbs of frequency to tell how often something happens or happened.
Writing Practice 125	Write ten sentences using adverbs of degree. Write two sentences with **very**, two with **really**, three with **so**, and three with **too.** Underline these words in your sentences.
Writing Practice 126	Write ten sentences with any ten of these words: **around, cloud, crowded, down, flower, found, house, how, loud, mountain, now, power, shout, town, vowel.** Underline these words in your sentences.
Writing Practice 127	Write ten sentences with any ten of these words: **about, allow, count, cow, flour, ground, hour, mouse, our, pound, shower, sound, sour, south, towel.** Underline these words in your sentences.
Writing Practice 128	Write five sentences with one word from Practice 126 and one word from Practice 127 in each sentence. Underline these words in your sentences.
Writing Practice 129	Write ten sentences about a place you really want to visit. Use adverbs in every sentence. (Hint: place, time, manner, frequency, degree)
Writing Practice 130	Write ten sentences about the daily routine of a person you know well. Use adverbs in every sentence. (Hint: place, time, manner, frequency, degree)

Unit 14

Writing Practice 131	Write ten sentences about what you are doing right now.
Writing Practice 132	Write ten sentences about what you are not doing right now.
Writing Practice 133	Write ten sentences about what your friends are doing right now.
Writing Practice 134	Write ten sentences about what your friends are not doing right now.
Writing Practice 135	Write ten sentences about animals at the zoo. Tell what they are doing right now.
Writing Practice 136	Write eight sentences with these eight words: **boy, choice, employer, enjoy, joy, noise, poison, toy.** Underline these words in your sentences.
Writing Practice 137	Write eight sentences with these eight words: **boil, coin, destroy, employee, join, oil, point, voice.** Underline these words in your sentences.
Writing Practice 138	Write five sentences with one word from Practice 136 and one word from Practice 137 in each sentence. Underline these words in your sentences.
Writing Practice 139	Write ten sentences with at least ten of the verbs in *29 Most Common Regular Past Tense Verbs in Writing* in Activity 1 (page 205). Use the present progressive tense of the verbs. Use at least five negative verbs.
Writing Practice 140	Write ten sentences about what a family is doing at a public park.

Appendix 3

Unit 1 Peer Editing Sheet Sample

This is an example of the Peer Editing Sheets available for *Great Writing: Foundations*. To print them, go to NGL.Cengage.com/GWF.

PEER EDITING 1

Your name: _____

Your partner's name: _____

Date: _____

1. How many sentences did you partner write? _____

2. Does every sentence begin with a capital letter? _____

   If not, copy the sentences here that need a capital letter.

   _____

   _____

3. Does every sentence end with a period? _____

   If not, copy the sentences here that need a period.

   _____

   _____

4. Does every sentence have a subject? _____

   If not, which sentences need a subject? Copy them here.

   _____

   _____

5. Does every sentence have a verb? _____

   If not, which sentences need a verb? Copy them here.

   _____

   _____

6. Does every sentence have correct word order? _____

   If not, copy the sentences here that do not have correct word order.

   _____

   _____

7. Copy a sentence that has the word **brother** or **sister**.

   _____

   _____

8. Copy the longest sentence here.

   _____

   _____

9. Are there any other mistakes? If so, write the mistake and the correction here.

	mistake	correction
1		
2		
3		

Appendix 4

The Parts of a Paragraph

What Is a Paragraph?

A **paragraph** is a group of sentences about **one** specific topic. A paragraph usually has three to ten sentences.

A paragraph is indented. This means there is a white space at the beginning of the first sentence.

Here is a group of sentences that can also be a paragraph.

Sentences	Paragraph
1. I have a big family.	indent↓
2. My name is Anna Sanders.	I have a big family. My name is Anna Sanders. I am twenty years old. I study English at my school. I have two brothers. I also have two sisters. I love my brothers and sisters a lot. We are a very happy family.
3. I am twenty years old.	
4. I study English at my school.	
5. I have two brothers.	
6. I also have two sisters.	
7. I love my brothers and sisters a lot.	
8. We are a very happy family.	

Parts of a Paragraph

A paragraph has three main parts: the topic sentence, the body, and a concluding sentence. See the example below that shows these parts.

1. **The Topic Sentence**

    Every good paragraph has a **topic sentence**. The topic sentence tells the main idea of the whole paragraph.

    The topic sentence:

    - is usually the first sentence in the paragraph.
    - should not be too specific or too general.

    If a paragraph does not have a topic sentence, the reader may not know what the paragraph is about. Make sure every paragraph has a topic sentence.

2. **The Body**

> Every good paragraph must have sentences that support the topic sentence. These supporting sentences are called the **body** of a paragraph.

The supporting sentences:

- give more information, such as details or examples, about the topic sentence.
- must be related to the topic sentence.

> A good body can make your paragraph stronger. You must be sure to cut out any unrelated or unconnected ideas.

3. **The Concluding Sentence**

> In addition to a topic sentence and body, every good paragraph has a **concluding sentence**. This sentence ends the paragraph with a final thought.

The concluding sentence:

- can give a summary of the information in the paragraph.
- can give information that is similar to the information in the topic sentence.
- can give a suggestion, an opinion, or a prediction.

topic sentence   the body

I have a big family. My name is Anna Sanders. I am twenty years old. I study English at

my school. I have two brothers. I also have two sisters. I love my brothers and sisters a lot.

concluding sentence (opinion)
We are a very happy family.

Index